Part of a project for HINDS Behavioral Health Services from funding provided by:

Recovery is a Process – Not an Outcome

This page left intentionally blank

BEHAVIORAL HEALTH MENTOR TRAINING

SECTION ONE 9
BEHAVIORAL HEALTH MENTOR TRAINING AGENDA 11
INTRODUCTION TO SECTION ONE 13
TRAINING OBJECTIVES 15

MODULE 1 16
CPSS 16
WHAT ARE THE COMPONENTS OF RECOVERY? 17
WHAT IS RECOVERY? 17
WHO AM I? 18
Exercise: Who Am I? 18
Exercise Who Am I? Lessons Learned – Summation 18
SPECTRUM OF ATTITUDES 19
How We Treat People 19
Treating People as Objects 19
Treating People as Recipients 19
Treating People as Resources 20
How have I Been Treating People? 20
VALUES AND DIFFERENCES 21
Exercise – Values Clarifications: About Differences 21
Values Clarifications 22

MODULE 2 23
STIGMA AND LABELS 23
The Power of Labels 23
Labels: Blocks to Recovery 23
STIGMA – A Definition 23
Words We Need to Abandon 23
Words We Need to Celebrate 23
SHARING YOUR STORY 24
Exercise: Sharing Your Story 24
Positive Use of Sharing Our Story 25

MODULE 3 26
ISSUES OF SELF-DISCLOSURE 26
Exercise: Self-Disclosure Scale 26
Questions of Self-Disclosure 27
CRISIS INTERVENTION 28
A Definition of Crisis 28
Crisis or No Crisis? 28
Possible Responses to an Immediate Crisis 28
Emergency Response to a Crisis 28

BEHAVIORAL HEALTH MENTOR TRAINING

- DE-ESCALATION 29
  - What is De-escalation? 29
  - So, a Few Things to Consider 30
  - Responses and Responsiveness 30
  - Five Surprises 31
  - 3 Guiding Principles for Every Situation 33
  - Summary 33

SECTION ONE SLIDES 34

SECTION TWO 47
- INTRODUCTION TO SECTION TWO 48
- TRAINING OBJECTIVES 49

MODULE 4 50
- FROM CO-OCCURRING DISORDER (COD) TO RECOVERY 50
- ROLES IN A FAMILY WITH CO-OCCURRING ISSUES 52
  - Substance Abuser 52
  - Chief Enabler 53
  - Family Hero 53
  - Family Scapegoat 54
  - Lost Child 55
  - Family Mascot 56
  - Exercise: Family Roles Discussion 56
- SILENTLY MARGINALIZED 57
  - Exercise – Family Imprisonment/ Silently Marginalization 57

MODULE 5 58
- EMOTIONAL BUTTONS 58
- EMOTIONAL BUTTONS DEFINED/IDENTIFIED 58
  - Exercise: Emotional Buttons 59
  - Understanding Your Responses 60
- DIFFERENTIATION AND UNDIFFERENTIATION 61
  - Family Systems: Bowen and differentiation 61
  - The Undifferentiated Self 61
  - Exercise: The Undifferentiated Self Part 1 61
  - Exercise: The Undifferentiated Self Part 2 61
  - The Well-Differentiated Self 62
  - Exercise: Un-Differentiated and Well-Differentiated 62
  - Bowen's "Differentiation of Self" 62
- CO-DEPENDENCY 63
  - Exercise: Family Restricted 63
  - Exercise: Defining Co-Dependency 63

BEHAVIORAL HEALTH MENTOR TRAINING

    Definition of Co-dependency 65
    Common Characteristics of Co-dependency 65
    Misconceptions About Co-dependency 65
    How a Co-dependent Relationship Develops 65
    The Development of the Co-dependent Self 66
  ENABLING 67
    How Do You Define Enabling? 67
    Exercise: Definition of Enabling 67
    Definition of Enabling 68
    Correlation between the Enabler and the Dual-diagnosed Person 68
    Progression of Enabling 68
        Stage One: Protection 68
        Stage Two: Controlling 68
        Stage Three: Super People or Martyr 68
    Why People Enable 69
    Personal Definition 69
    Three C's about Chemical Dependency and Co-occurring Disorders 69

MODULE 6 70
  RECOVERY – HEALTHY FAMILY 70
    From Co-Dependency to Interdependency 70
    Healthy Interdependency 70
    To Recovery and a Healthy Family 70
    A Happy Family in Recovery 71
    The Long Road out of Co-dependency into Recovery 71
    Family Responses to a Co-occurring Disordered Person Clean and Well 71
    Exercise: Family Response to Recovery 71
    How to Support a Newly Recovering Family 72
    What is Detachment? 72
    Traits of a Healthy Family 72
    Exercise – Traits of a Healthy Family 72
  FAMILY SCULPTING 74
    Definition of Family Sculpting 74
    Family Sculpting 74
    Exercise – Your Family Sculpture 77

SECTION TWO SLIDES 78

SECTION THREE 99
  INTRODUCTION TO SECTION THREE 100
  TRAINING OBJTECTIVES 101

MODULE 7 102

BEHAVIORAL HEALTH MENTOR TRAINING

- ETHICS 102
  - What Are Ethics? 102
  - Ethics – A Definition 103
  - Exercise: Principle, Morals, Values 103
  - Some Common Definitions 104
  - Ethics in Recovery Coaching and Peer Support Specialist Mentoring 104
  - Stay in Your Lane 105
  - Exercise: Boundaries 106
  - Core Recovery Values and Ethical Conduct 107
- FRAGILITY 109
- FRAGILITY OF POST-TREATMENT RECOVERY 110

MODULE 8 111
- CULTURE AND CULTURAL COMPETENCE 111
  - Definition of Culture 112
  - Definition of Cultural Competence 112
- POWER SHUFFLE 113
- MEDICATION MANAGEMENT 114
  - What is MedTEAM? 114
  - Practice Principles of MedTEAM 114
  - Informed Medication Decisions 114
  - Team Approach 115
  - Medication-Related Outcomes 115
  - High-Quality Documentation 115
  - Shared Decision Making 115
  - Systematic Plan for Medication Management 116

MODULE 9 117
- LIVE YOUR LIFE NOT YOUR STORY 117
  - The Story – The Past 118
  - Holistic 118
  - Triune Synergistic Model 119
  - The Synergy That Is Life 119
  - Quotes Reflecting Bringing Consciousness in the Moment 121
- SELF-CARE 122
  - Wellness Self-Assessment 122
  - Physical Wellness Self-Assessment 122
  - Emotional/Psychological Wellness Self-Assessment 122
  - Spiritual Wellness Self-Assessment 122
  - Intellectual Wellness Self-Assessment 123
  - Occupational Wellness Self-Assessment 123
  - Social Wellness Self-Assessment 123
  - Environmental Wellness Self-Assessment 123
- SAMHSA – PERSONAL AND FAMILY WELLNESS 124

BEHAVIORAL HEALTH MENTOR TRAINING

- Exercise – What is Wellness? ... 124
- Definition of Wellness ... 125
- Aspects of Wellness ... 125
- 8 Dimensions of SAMSHA's Wellness Initiative ... 125
- Why Wellness Matters ... 126
- PERSONAL WELLNESS ... 127
- THE RECOVERY WELLNESS PLAN ... 128
- RECOVERY WELLNESS PLAN (*For the Recoveree*) ... 129

SECTION THREE SLIDES ... 139

APPENDIX ... 157

JOURNAL PAGES ... 158

ALL RECOVERY MEETING ... 163

BIOGRAPHIES ... 164

ACKNOWLEDGEMENTS ... 168

Materials and slides compiled and presented from work by:

Connecticut Community for Addiction Recovery
Russell Gillette, LM, HC
Murray Bowen, Ph.D.
Richard D Dávila, Ph.D.
Michael M Galer, DBA
Jackie Sue Griffin, MBA, MS
Mitch Ablett, Ph. D
Terry Gorski, MS
Marguerite "Rita" Ballard, CRRA, RC, RFM
Right Response - http://rightresponse.org/my/

Contributions from:

HINDS BEHAVIORAL HEALTH SERVICES

Dr. Kathy Crockett, Ph. D, Ph.D., MPH, LPC-S, LCMHT Executive Director
Pamela Coker, LCSW Director of Adult Services

TRAINER OF TRAINERS (TOT)

Ekoko Onema
Jessica James
Linda White
Monica Wolters
Marci Kinchen

TURNAROUND LIFE

Peter Gamache, Ph.D.
Jackie Sue Griffin, MBA, MS
Logan Nalker, Research Assistant

RECOVERY ALL

Richard D Davila, Ph.D.
Nydia Orozco–Davila, MS, MSW
Marguerite "Rita" Ballard, CRRA, RC, RFM

SECTION ONE

This page left intentionally blank

BEHAVIORAL HEALTH MENTOR TRAINING AGENDA

SECTION ONE
- Introductions
- Working Agreements
- Training Objectives
- Section One Agenda
- Module 1
  - CPSS
  - Who Am I?
  - Spectrum of Attitudes
  - Values and Differences
- Module 2
  - Stigma and Labels
  - Sharing Your Story
  - Issues of Self-Disclosure
- Module 3
  - Crisis Intervention
  - De-escalation
  - All Recovery Meeting

SECTION TWO
- Welcome, Agenda and Reconnection
- Training Objectives
- Module 4
  - Co-occurring Disorder to Recovery
  - Roles in a Family
  - Silently Marginalized
- Module 5
  - Emotional Buttons
  - Differentiation and Un-differentiation
  - Codependency
  - Enabling
- Module 6
  - Family Reaction to Recovery
  - Traits of a Healthy Family
  - Family Sculpting
  - All Recovery Meeting

SECTION THREE
- Welcome, Agenda and Reconnection
- Module 7
  - Ethics
  - Fragility
- Module 8
  - Defining Culture and Cultural Competence
  - Power Shuffle
  - Medication Management
- Module 9
  - Live Your Life Not Your Story
  - Self-Care
  - Recovery Wellness Plan
  - All Recovery Meeting

AT THE END OF EACH SECTION, ARE THE SLIDES USED WHEN THE TRAINING IS CONDUCTED ON-SITE.

INTRODUCTION TO SECTION ONE

In this section, we include three modules. We start with what is a Certified Peer Support Specialist (CPSS), Definition and Components of Recovery, Who Am I, and Spectrum of Attitudes, Values and Differences. It is intentionally presented so that we can understand the definition of a CPSS so that we can start acquiring more knowledge and skills to make this role work.

"Who Am I" is an exercise that helps us look into who and what our support groups are. We explore who and what these are within us and write them down. We then name them within a pie chart given each one the size slice that is appropriate. Then we ask someone to arbitrarily cross out two of them. The point of this exercise is to point out that as Helper we sometimes discount the importance of what is a support group for another person especially a person with a co-occurring disorder.

Spectrum of Attitudes is a description of how we treat people. William Lofquist in his book "Discovering the Meaning of Prevention: A Practical Approach to Positive Change", describes three distinct ways that people can be treated. Either as an Object, a Recipient or a Resource. We go on and then to describe what these are as well ask the participant or the reader to reflect on their lives and share an experience when they were treated as an object, recipient or a resource. Right after this, we present Values and Differences. This where we get a chance to reflect on what might be our biases. This is important to find out because we must be aware of this before we can implement a change within ourselves.

We go on to discuss Stigma and Labels. This is a major barrier to admitting the problem. This is so for both the person with co-occurring disorder and the family. This will be discussed along with an exercise.

Another piece presented here is the pros and cons of Sharing Your Story. When is it appropriate for the Helper to share their story and when is not? Right after this, we present Issues of Self-Disclosure, which is a follow-up to sharing your story.

We end this section with Crisis Intervention and De-escalation. What is a crisis and what is not a crisis? We present this with an exercise responding to the above question.

There are different definitions of de-escalation, however with very similar wording. We chose to use the one below because it appeared to synthesize most of the definitions we came across. **De-escalation** refers to behavior that is intended to escape escalations of conflicts. It may also refer to approaches in conflict resolution. Escalations of commitment are often hard from spiraling out of proportions without specific measures being taken. *(Wikipedia)*

As the reader can see, we begin with a clarification of the role of a Peer Support Specialist and continue to reflect through exercises the loss of support groups by an insensitive Helper and then on to examining how we treat people by reflecting some of our experiences on how we, at times, have been treated by others. Finally examining, Crisis Intervention and De-escalation and some actions that should help reduce the client's agitation and potential for future aggression or violence.

We hope you can get some direction from the way material is presented here.

……Peace……

TRAINING OBJECTIVES

SECTION ONE:

Module 1
- CPSS
- Who Am I?
- Spectrum of Attitudes
- Values and Differences

Module 2
- Stigma and Labels
- Sharing Your Story

Module 3
- Issues of Self-Disclosure
- Crisis Intervention
- De-escalation

Module 1
CPSS

Who Are Certified Peer Support Specialists and What Do They Do?

Because of his or her lived experience, a CPSS has knowledge and skills that professional training cannot replicate. The hallmark of peer support is not so much what kind of service is provided, but who provides it and how.

The "who" must be a person with lived experience of mental illness and/or substance abuse. The "how" must be built on the values and principles of peer support.

A Certified Peer Support Specialist

Is/Does	Is Not/Does Not
A person in recovery	A professional clinician
Share lived experience	Give professional clinical advice
A role model	An expert or authority figure
See whole individuals in the context of their community	See an individual as a case role, family and/or diagnosis
Motivate through hope and inspiration	Motivate through fear or negative consequences
Support many pathways to recovery	Recommend one specific pathway to recovery
Function as an advocate for the person in recovery, both within and outside of the program.	Represent perspectives of the program
Helps foster independence	Help foster dependence
Teach how to access needed resources	Provide basic necessities, such as place to live, money, etc.
Use language based on common experiences	Use clinical language
Share knowledge of local resources	Provide case management services
Help set personal goals	Mandate tasks and behaviors
Provide one-on-one recovery support	Tell a person how to lead his/her life in recovery

Source: Substance Abuse and Mental Health Services Administration (SAMSHA)

WHAT ARE THE COMPONENTS OF RECOVERY?

Strengths-Based:

Recovery focuses on valuing and building on the multiple capacities, resiliencies, talents, coping abilities, and inherent worth of individuals. By building on these strengths, consumers leave stymied life roles behind and engage in new life roles (e.g., partner, caregiver, friend, student, employee).

The process of recovery moves forward through interaction with others in supportive, trust-based relationships

WHAT IS RECOVERY?

Recovery is a process of change through which individuals improve their health and wellness, live a self-directed life, and strive to reach their full potential.

WHO AM I?

Discovering the "I" in the BHM Process

Exercise: Who Am I?

Describe yourself: Include things like your name, ethnicity, gender, marital/partner status, occupation, hobbies, interests, accomplishments, hopes, dreams and goals.

Son of God, Missionary for Christ, Single-white-male, Servant, Mecanic, artist, student, fantasy, faith, family, Sobriey and Recovery, Prison Outreach and Ministy, Alive Again, Music, Cooking,

Using the list above, create all the "groups" or roles than you feel represent, influence and matter to you

Son of God
Missionary for Christ
Student / Servant
artist
Mecanic
faith
family
Recovery

Of the groups/roles you identified, choose the five that are the most important to your perception of who you are.

Son of God
Missionary for Christ
Servant
Student
Recovery

Use a pie chart to represent how those five groups/roles represent you

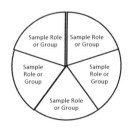

Exercise Who Am I? Lessons Learned – Summation

One of the lessons of this exercise is to illustrate what it feels like when someone negates a part of what defines you.

SPECTRUM OF ATTITUDES

How We Treat People

William Lofquist describes how we treat people in three ways: as objects, as recipients, as resources.

Treating People as Objects

We treat people as an Object when:
- We know what is best for them and we are going to decide for them
- We know where someone needs to go and we are going to take them there
- We give them no say in the matter
  (taking a hostage)

Our culture is filled with examples of people treating us as objects. Educational systems often treat us as objects as do health care systems. We often feel we have limited control over where we are headed and/or what happens to us.

Please take time to reflect when you were being treated as an *Object* and write this down in the space provided.

FDC

Treating People as Recipients

We treat people as a Recipient when we still believe that we know what is best for someone but …
- We "give" them the opportunity to participate in the decision-making because it will be "good" for them or for the group.
- They are supposed to receive the benefits of what we give to them
- The recipient may figure out that decisions have already been made

Please take time to reflect when you were being treated as a *Recipient* and write this down in the space provided.

Salvation Army ARC

Treating People as Resources

We treat people as Resources when there is the attitude of respect by the first person or group toward what the other person or group can do.

This attitude and the behaviors that follow it can be closely associated with two matters of great concern: self-esteem and productivity. Creating a culture in which people are viewed as resources, is a worthy goal

Please take time to reflect when you were being treated as a **Resource** and write this down in the space provided.

Alive Again

How have I Been Treating People?

For most people, being treated as an object or recipient is a negative experience, while being treated as a resource most often elicits positive feelings.

The lesson for us here is when we are helping others as a Recovery Family Mentor, it is important to treat people as resources as much as possible. People are the experts of their experience. They may need help in knowing about or accessing resources, but the choice should always be theirs.

Please take time to reflect when you treated someone as an **Object**, **Recipient** or **Resource** and write this down in the space provided.

My spousee and mentee is treated as both recipient and resource

VALUES AND DIFFERENCES

Family conflict can arise by not understanding things such as, generational differences, sibling rivalry and of course many other possibilities.

The national lead agency, Substance Abuse and Mental Health Services Administration, (SAMHSA) (www.samhsa.gov) states one of the strongest forms of continued successful recovery for substance use disorder, when leaving treatment, is continual family support.

How do we get past the family conflicts to be a positive support resource? One way is looking at our values, particularly those about differences among people.

Exercise – Values Clarifications: About Differences

1. What are some of the attributes of the people you find yourself drawn to?

    Integrity, honesty, dependability, and loyalty

2. What are some of the attributes of the people you tend to avoid?

    dishonesty, Prideful, ego driven, carnality

3. Describe the thinking process you go through when someone disagrees with or challenges you? How do you feel when this happens?

    I leave changing minds to God.

4. How did you discover that people were different on the basis of race, ethnicity and culture? How did you discover that some races, ethnic groups and cultures are considered negative by others?

    life.

5. Describe your most common feelings when you encounter people different from yourself. How do these feelings affect your interactions with them?

    I am usually intriged and want to know more about them. It makes me a more active participant in the relationship.

Values Clarifications

- It's natural to have an affinity for some and not for others
- Pretending we like all people the same doesn't allow for us to watch our verbal and non-verbal behaviors to make sure we are treating all people equally
- Many of our values are deep-seeded and come from early life experiences
- We need to be honest about our biases and work to overcome them

We need to remember it is not a peer support specialist with biases that is a concern, because we all have biases. The real concern is a peer support specialist who believes that he/she does not have any biases because:
- this makes it impossible to watch for any biases and how they may be harming interactions with someone.
- this may occur sometimes when one person is favored over another.

Module 2

STIGMA AND LABELS

The Power of Labels

William White argues that Language can:
- Empower OR dis-empower
- Humanize OR objectify
- Engender compassion OR fear and hatred
- Motivate OR deflate
- Comfort OR wound
- Unite OR create enmity

Labels: Blocks to Recovery

"Reducing a person to nothing more than their difficulties is one of the most damaging and dehumanizing forms of language. It denies the existence of any facet of the person, any relevant roles or characteristics, other than their diagnosis" - *Perkins & Repper (2001)*

STIGMA – A Definition

Webster defines stigma as "a mark of shame or discredit"

Modern culture has used labels to denote devalued social categories. The labels influence public perceptions and behaviors and serve to:
- Devalue and diminish
- Denigrate
- Discriminate

Stigma robs people of rightful life opportunities
Stigma interacts with illness and exposes people to distorted experiences with criminal/mental health/medical treatment
Stigma leads health care systems to "withhold appropriate services"

Words We Need to Abandon

Abuse *Self-help* *Consumer*
Untreated Alcoholic/Addict/Gambler/Dual-Diagnosed Person

Words We Need to Celebrate

Recovery *Advocacy* *Sustainability*
Recovery Support Services *Recovery Coach/Mentor* *Peer Advocate/Mentor Recovery*
Community *Recovery Pathway/Style*

Adapted from William White

SHARING YOUR STORY

Exercise: Sharing Your Story

This is a common expression for people in recovery, but we all have a story whether or not we are in recovery.

Please answer the five questions in the exercise from the perspective of a Peer Support Specialist.

1. What does "sharing your story" mean to you?

2. When you share your story, what do you usually include?

3. List several situations where sharing your story would be a positive endeavor.

4. List several situations where sharing your story would have negative implications.

5. What are some of the factors that change sharing your story from a positive experience to a negative experience?

Positive Use of Sharing Our Story

- Your sessions with a recoveree are about them and not you
- Keep your own story brief and with a purpose
- Use your story to show empathy, illustrate an example, or describe a choice and its' consequences
- Remember that parts of your story may raise uncomfortable feelings for someone who has not yet dealt with past difficulties

Module 3
ISSUES OF SELF-DISCLOSURE

Exercise: Self-Disclosure Scale

This exercise is going to lead us to a broader look at issues of self-disclosure.

Indicate how helpful or harmful you think it would be to share each statement within the context of a recovery mentoring session. Before each number, write the number on the continuum (1-5) that best represents your thoughts about the appropriateness of that self-disclosure. Respond according to your own beliefs rather than to the way others might respond. Also, respond as if the disclosure were true for you.

      1 = very helpful
      2 = helpful
      3 = not helpful
      4 = harmful
      5 = very harmful

Topics I might share with the recoveree:

_____ 1. Feelings of anxiety or uncertainty about what's happening in the conversation.

_____ 2. Doubts about my confidence in being a coach/mentor/support person.

_____ 3. Doubts about my expertise in some of the material I am talking about.

_____ 4. Anger towards someone I am coaching/mentoring/supporting.

_____ 5. Feeling happy about the progress we are making.

_____ 6. Special feelings or connections with someone I am coaching/mentoring/supporting.

_____ 7. That I am HIV positive.

_____ 8. That I am bi-polar.

_____ 9. The admission that I have conflicts with the recovery process of the person I am coaching/mentoring/supporting.

_____ 10. My boredom with someone I am coaching/mentoring/supporting.

Questions of Self-Disclosure

- Ask yourself who is being served by the self-disclosure (it should be the recoveree who is being served)
- Don't self-disclose as a means to short-cut a recoveree's discovery process
- Be careful of disclosing a traumatic incident from your own life if you have no knowledge of how the self-disclosure will be received

CRISIS INTERVENTION

A Definition of Crisis
An event that poses immediate safety concerns to the degree that they would need some resolution by the end of the coaching session.

Crisis or No Crisis?

_____ the recoveree shares that there is not enough money to pay all of the bills

_____ the recoveree is having suicidal ideation

_____ the recoveree comes to the coaching session drunk

_____ the recoveree is despondent over the break-up of a relationship

_____ the recoveree shares that they were sexually abused as a child

_____ the recoveree is abnormally anxious and can't sit still

_____ the recoveree is angry because the person they asked to be their sponsor said no

_____ the recoveree discusses wanting to physically hurt someone

Possible Responses to an Immediate Crisis
- call 911
- call for immediate help from a coworker, supervisor
- emergency medical treatment
- do not let the person be alone
- do not let the person drive
- get the recoveree to call for help from a professional they have been seeing

Emergency Response to a Crisis
- Seek immediate help in an emergency crisis
- Report someone who is dangerous, threatening, violent, self-harming, destructive or suicidal
- Support safety first
- Involve others, particularly 911
- Report the incident and response to a supervisor

DE-ESCALATION

Material adapted from Article: De-escalate Anyone, Anywhere, Anytime[SM]
Unplug the Power Struggle with Principle-Based De-escalation (http://rightresponse.org/my/)

What is De-escalation?

Helping someone who is escalated to restabilize back to their Baseline state so that they can manage their own needs.

Despite the importance of de-escalation in promoting a non-coercive psychiatric environment, a review of the literature conducted by Mavandadi, Bieling and Madsen (2016) identified only 19 articles that defined or provided a model of de-escalation and below is the consensus of that study.

1. **Valuing the client:** Provides genuine acknowledgement that the client's concerns are valid, important and will be addressed in a meaningful way.
2. **Reducing fear:** Listens actively to the client and offers genuine empathy while suggesting that the client's situation has the potential for positive future change.
3. **Inquiring about client's queries and anxiety:** Can communicate a thorough understanding of the client's concerns and works to uncover the root of the issue.
4. **Providing guidance to the client:** Suggests multiple ways to the help the client with their current concerns and recommends preventative measures.
5. **Working out possible agreements:** Takes responsibility for the client's care and concludes the encounter with an agreed-upon short-term solution and a long-term action plan.
6. **Remaining calm:** Maintains a calm tone of voice and steady pace that is appropriate to the client's feelings and behavior.

7. **Risky:** Maintains a moderate distance from the client to ensure safety but does not appear guarded and fearful.

While no single technique will work on every person, there is a small set of principles that do apply to everyone. These principles are universal, so they apply to any age person, any level of ability or disability, and any setting.

So, a Few Things to Consider

- Escalation time is not teaching time.
- This is not a good time for discussion.
- Remember how your thinking brain gets turned off when you are escalated? You must remember that the escalated person has a similar mindset.
- When their thinking brain is off, you have to appeal to their survival brain.

Responses and Responsiveness

Negotiating with an escalated person will likely be unproductive, if they are truly escalated. If you are able to negotiate with the person, they are probably not that escalated. their responsiveness is a reflection of their escalation. If they cannot make any sense out of what you are doing or saying, that is a sign of their escalation. Their response is feedback for you and how you should respond.

There are studies that show that a physical response to physical aggression actually increases the likelihood that physical aggression will occur again. If you have to protect yourself or physically intervene, it should not be for the purpose of behavior management, compliance, punishment or even to vent your own frustrations. Physical intervention should only be used for safety protection.

Five Surprises

1. **Manage yourself first before managing others**
During an airline safety briefing you are instructed when the mask drops to first place it on yourself before assisting anyone else. *Why? You've got to take care of yourself before you can take care of anyone else.*

   When hearing "remain in control of a situation", many assume that means that you control the situation by controlling the other person. The surprise here is that in order to manage others, you must first manage yourself.

   We cannot control others, we can only control ourselves. The way we remain in control of a situation is by controlling ourselves. The paradox here is that when you change your own behavior, you change the outcome of the situation.

2. **One response does not fit all**
A common misconception of de-escalation skills is that you can learn a specific technique and it will always deescalate the person in front of you. It is not uncommon to hear people say, "I usually do _____, but this one time it didn't work."

   The same technique will not always work because different people have different needs. You can even take the same two people and the same issue, and the situation may resolve differently on a different day. You will be most effective when you can adapt in the moment to the needs of the person you're trying to support. *the only response that works every time is the right response for that specific situation*

   Many people stick to just one response because that is the one tool they are comfortable using. Or, they continually use the same response because they are still using the same old map.
"One response does not fit all" may seem obvious in writing but ask around and see for yourself how many tools people keep in their *de-escalation toolbox*.

3. **Making it stop does not make it stop**
We have to remember that behavior is a form of communication. It may not always be a good form, but it is a valid form of communication. Human nature drives people to get their needs met in whatever ways possible. To understand what a person is communicating, we not only have to listen to their words but also "listen" to their behavior and their body language.
   Two Fundamental Questions:
   1. *"What is this person trying to gain?"*
   2. *"What is this person trying to avoid?"*

4. **Postvention Prevents Problems**

Prevention is the preparation before an event to ensure it doesn't happen. **Postvention** is what you learn after an event that allows you to prevent it from happening again. Maybe you were unable to foresee or prevent this incident from happening this time, but what you learn from this incident you can use to prevent it from occurring in the future.

Postvention prevents problems because you can only prevent something from occurring when you can foresee it. This means you need to *assess what has already occurred* and decide what should happen next time. This is a critical turning point in always having the right response. You are most likely to know what to do in an event when you have already planned for it. In a long-term approach, this will be your most critical work.

5. **Inside-Out Change** - *Changing your way of thinking and responding to make a difference in the situation at hand.*

Inside-Out Change is a significant de-escalation strategy. It comes from within and reflects the change you make regarding the situation. Earlier, it was mentioned that the goal of always being in control of a situation. It turns out that *if you can change your thinking about a situation, you can change the outcome.*

Inside-out change requires confidence, empowerment, leadership and a desire to shift toward long-term relationships. Inside-out change requires both personal and professional leadership.

Inside-out change requires the willingness to provide people with knowledge, skills and support.

Inside-out change requires that we sacrifice our personal priorities and comforts in the service of those in need.

3 Guiding Principles for Every Situation

How is it possible to always have the right response? During an incident you may not always know exactly what to do, but *3 Guiding Principles will always guide your actions in any situation.*

1. **Meet the needs** of the person that you're dealing with. Meet their individual needs, their needs in that moment as well as their long-term needs.
2. **Reflect respect and dignity** toward the people you're dealing with. No matter what this person is calling you or how they are inconveniencing you, the lack of dignity or respect will not help you productively resolve the situation.
3. It is always the right response to **maintain the safety of everyone** involved.

How do you always have the right response? These 3 Guiding Principles will help you in any situation. Not sure what to do? Take a little test:

- Will my response meet the **needs** of the person?
- Is my response **respectful** and dignified?
- Will my response maintain **safety**?

If yes, that is probably the right response. If your response does not meet these 3 goals, it is probably the wrong response. Remember that **the wrong response is likely to increase the escalation**, increase the risk of somebody getting hurt and negatively impact your relationship with that person.

This is the core essence of what it will take to always have the right response. The rest is experience, skills and tips. You cannot always have the right response unless you are ready for inside-out change and prepared to follow these **3 Guiding Principles**.

Summary

Five Surprises
1. Manage yourself first before managing others
2. One response does not fit all
3. Making it stop does not make it stop
4. Postvention Prevents Problems
5. Inside-Out Change

Three Guiding Principles for Every Situation
1. Needs
2. Respect
3. Safety

Remain in control always. Support anyone, anywhere, with any issue   Avoid the wrong response which can make the situation worse.

SECTION ONE SLIDES

Behavioral Health Mentor Training
Section One

This program was created through Recovery All by:

Richard D Dávila
and
Marguerite "Rita" Ballard

Introductions

- Name
- From where
- Recovery status
  (in recovery, family member, friend of recovery)
- Motivation for being a part of this process

Working Agreements

Overview

SECTION ONE

- Introductions
- Working Agreements
- Training Objectives
- Section One Agenda
- Module 1
  - CPSS
  - Who Am I?
  - Spectrum of Attitudes
  - Values and Differences

SECTION ONE

- Module 2
  - Stigma and Labels
  - Sharing Your Story
  - Issues of Self-Disclosure
- Module 3
  - Crisis Intervention
  - De-escalation
- **All Recovery Meeting**

SECTION TWO

- Welcome, Agenda and Reconnection
- Training Objectives
- Module 4
  - Co-occurring Disorder to Recovery
  - Roles in a Family
  - Silently Marginalized

SECTION TWO

- Module 5
  - Emotional Buttons
  - Differentiation and Un-differentiation
  - Codependency
  - Enabling
- Module 6
  - Family Reaction to Recovery
  - Traits of a Healthy Family
  - Family Sculpting
- **All Recovery Meeting**

SECTION THREE

- Welcome, Agenda and Reconnection
- Module 7
  - Ethics
  - Fragility
- Module 8
  - Defining Cultural and Cultural Competence
  - Power Shuffle
  - Medication Management
- Module 9
  - Live Your Life Not Your Story
  - Self-Care
  - Recovery Wellness Plan
- **All Recovery Meeting**

Today's Agenda

- Introduction
- Working Agreements
- Overview
- Today's Agenda
- Module 1
  - CPSS
  - Who Am I?
  - Spectrum of Attitudes

Today's Agenda

- Module 2
  - Stigma and Labels
  - Sharing Your Story
- Module 3
  - Issues of Self-Disclosure
  - Crisis Intervention & De-escalation
- **All Recovery Meeting**

CPSS

Who are Certified Peer Support Specialists and what do they do?

- Because of his or her lived experience, a CPSS has knowledge and skills that professional training cannot replicate.
- The hallmark of peer support is not so much what kind of service is provided, but who provides it and how.
- The "who" must be a person with lived experience of mental illness and/or substance abuse.
- The "how" must be built on the values and principles of peer support.

Certified Peer Support Specialist

Is/Does	Is Not/Does Not
A person in recovery	A professional clinician
Share lived experience	Give professional clinical advice
A role model	An expert or authority figure
See whole individuals in the context of their community	See an individual as a case roles, family and /or diagnosis
Motivate through hope and inspiration	Motivate through fear or negative consequences
Support many pathways to recovery	Recommend one specific pathway to recovery

---

Certified Peer Support Specialist

Is/Does	Is Not/Does Not
Function as an advocate for the person in recovery, both within and outside of the program.	Represent perspectives of the program
Helps foster independence	Help foster dependence
Teach how to access needed resources	Provide basic necessities, such as place to live, money, etc.
Use language based on common experiences	Use clinical language
Share knowledge of local resources	Provide case management services
Help set personal goals	Mandate tasks and behaviors
Provide one-on-one recovery support	Tell a person how to lead his/her life in recovery

Source: Substance Abuse and Mental Health Services Administration (SAMSHA)

WHAT ARE THE COMPONENTS OF RECOVERY?

STRENGTHS-BASED:

- Recovery focuses on valuing and building on the multiple capacities, resiliencies, talents, coping abilities, and inherent worth of individuals.
- By building on these strengths, consumers leave stymied life roles behind and engage in new life roles (e.g., partner, caregiver, friend, student, employee).
- The process of recovery moves forward through interaction with others in supportive, trust-based relationships

WHAT IS RECOVERY?

Recovery is a process of change through which individuals improve their health and wellness, live a self directed life, and strive to reach their full potential.

Exercise: Who Am I?

Describe yourself. Include things like your name, ethnicity, gender, marital/partner status, occupation, hobbies, interests, accomplishments, hopes, dreams and goals.

List all of the "groups" or roles that you feel represent, influence and matter to you.

Of the groups/roles you identified, choose five that are the most important to your perception of who you are.

Use a pie chart to represent how those five groups/roles represent you.

Spectrum of Attitudes

How We Treat People

William Lofquist describes how we treat people in three ways:
- As objects
- As recipients
- As resources

We Treat People as Objects When...

- We know what's best for them and we're going to decide for them
- We know where someone needs to go and we're going to take them there
- We give them no say in the matter
  (taking a hostage)

Please take time to reflect when you were being treated as an *Object* and write this in your manual.

Exercise: Treated as an Object

Discuss within your group one time when you felt you were viewed as an object and how you felt about it.

We Treat People as Recipients When…

- We still know what's best for someone but …
  - We "give" them the opportunity to participate in the decision-making because it'll be "good" for them or for the group
  - They're supposed to receive the benefits of what we give to them
  - They may figure out or feel that the decision has already been made

Please take time to reflect when you were being treated as a *Recipient* and write this in your manual.

Exercise: Treated as a Recipient

Discuss within your group one time when you felt you were viewed as an recipient and how you felt about it.

We Treat People as Resources When…

- There is an attitude of respect by the first person or group toward what the other person or group can do

This attitude can be closely associated with two matters of great concern: self-esteem and productivity. Creating a culture in which people are viewed as resources, is a worthy goal.

Please take time to reflect when you were being treated as a *Resource* and write this in your manual.

Exercise: Treated as a Resource

Discuss within your group one time when you felt you were viewed as an resource and how you felt about it.

How Have I Been Treating People?

- For most people, being treated as an object or recipient is a negative experience, while being treated as a resource most often elicits positive feelings.

- As a Behavioral Health Mentor, it is important to treat people as resources as much as possible

Please take time to reflect when you treated someone as an *Object*, *Recipient* or *Resource* and write this in your handout.

Values and Differences

We are going to proceed with an exercise that begins to look at our values, particularly those that are about differences among people.

Please take time to write down your answers to the five questions in the exercise in your manuals. You will do this individually.

Exercise: Values Clarifications About Differences

1. What are some of the attributes of the people you find yourself drawn to?
2. What are some of the attributes of the people you tend to avoid?
3. Describe the thinking process you go through when someone disagrees with or challenges you? How do you feel when this happens?
4. How did you discover that people were different on the basis of race, ethnicity and culture? How did you discover that some races, ethnic groups and cultures are considered negative by others?
5. Describe your most common feelings when you encounter people different from yourself. How do these feelings affect your interactions with them?

Values Clarification

- It's natural to have an affinity for some and not for others
- Pretending we like all people the same doesn't allow for us to watch our verbal and non-verbal behaviors to make sure we are treating all people equally
- Many of our values are deep-seated and come from early life experiences
- We need to be honest about our biases and work to overcome them

Concerns about Biases

- It is not a support mentor with biases that is a concern, because we all have biases
- The real concern is a support mentor who believes that he/she doesn't have any biases because:
  - This makes it impossible to watch for any biases and how they may be harming our interaction with someone
  - This may occur in families when one person is favored over another

Stigma and Labels

The Power of Labels

- William White argues that Language can:
  - Empower OR dis-empower
  - Humanize OR objectify
  - Engender compassion OR fear and hatred
  - Motivate OR deflate
  - Comfort OR wound
  - Unite OR create enmity

Labels: Blocks to Recovery

"Reducing a person to nothing more than their difficulties is one of the most damaging and dehumanizing forms of language. It denies the existence of any facet of the person, any relevant roles or characteristics, other than their diagnosis"

Perkins & Repper (2001)

Stigma

Webster defines stigma as "a mark of shame or discredit"

Stigma

- Modern culture has used labels to denote devalued social categories
- The labels influence public perceptions and behaviors and serve to:
  - Devalue and diminish
  - Denigrate
  - Discriminate

Wahl (1999)

Stigma

- Stigma robs people of rightful life opportunities
- Stigma interacts with illness and exposes people to distorted experiences with criminal/mental health/medical treatment
- Stigma leads health care systems to "withhold appropriate services"

Corrigan and Kleinlein

Words We Need to Abandon

- Abuse
- Self-help
- Untreated Alcoholic/Addict/Gambler/Dual-Diagnosed Person
- Consumer

Adopted from White

Words to Celebrate

- Recovery
- Recovery Community
- Advocacy
- Sustainability
- Recovery Support Services
- Recovery Coach/Mentor
- Peer Advocate/Mentor
- Recovery Pathway/Style

Adopted from White

Sharing Your Story

Sharing Your Story

This is a common expression for people in recovery, but we all have a story whether or not we are in recovery.

Please answer the five questions in the exercise from the perspective of a Behavioral Health Mentor.

Exercise

- What does "sharing your story" mean to you?
- When you share your story, what do you usually include?
- List several situations where sharing your story would be a positive endeavor.
- List several situations where sharing your story would have negative implications.
- What are some of the factors that change sharing your story from a positive experience to a negative experience?

Positive Use of Sharing Our Story

- Your sessions with a recoveree are about them and not you
- Keep your own story brief and with a purpose
- Use your story to show empathy, illustrate an example, or describe a choice and its' consequences
- Remember that parts of your story may raise uncomfortable feelings for someone who has not yet dealt with past difficulties

Issues of Self-Disclosure

Exercise: Self-Disclosure Scale

This exercise is going to lead us to a broader look at issues of self-disclosure.

- Take a look at the situations listed in this exercise in the manual.
- After thinking about each one, indicate how helpful or harmful you think it would be to share each statement within the context of a recovery mentoring session.
- Before each number, write the number on the continuum (1-5) that best represents your thoughts about the appropriateness of that self-disclosure.
- Respond according to your own beliefs rather than to the way others might respond.
- Also, respond as if the disclosure were true for you.

Questions of Self-Disclosure

- Ask yourself who is being served by the self-disclosure (it should be the recoveree who is being served)
- Don't self-disclose as a means to short-cut a recoveree's discovery process
- Be careful of disclosing a traumatic incident from your own life if you have no knowledge of how the self-disclosure will be received

Crisis Intervention

Crisis

An event that poses immediate safety concerns to the degree that they would need some resolution by the end of the support session.

Crisis or No Crisis

- the recoveree shares that there is not enough money to pay all of the bills
- the recoveree is having suicidal ideation
- the recoveree comes to the coaching session drunk
- the recoveree is despondent over the break-up of a relationship
- the recoveree shares that they were sexually abused as a child
- the recoveree is abnormally anxious and can't sit still
- the recoveree is angry because the person they asked to be their sponsor said no
- the recoveree discusses wanting to physically hurt someone

Possible Responses to an Immediate Crisis

- call 911
- call for immediate help from a coworker, supervisor
- emergency medical treatment
- do not let the person be alone
- do not let the person drive
- get the recoveree to call for help from a professional they have been seeing

Emergency Response to a Crisis

- Seek immediate help in an emergency crisis
- Report someone who is dangerous, threatening, violent, self-harming, destructive or suicidal
- Support safety first
- Involve others, particularly 911
- Report the incident and response to a supervisor

De-escalation

Material adapted from Article: De-escalate Anyone, Anywhere, Anytime℠ Unplug the Power Struggle with Principle-Based De-escalation (http://rightresponse.org/my/)

De-escalation

- Helping someone who is escalated to restabilize back to their Baseline state so that they can manage their own needs.
- While no single technique will work on every person, there is a small set of principles that do apply to everyone.
- These principles are universal, so they apply to any age person, any level of ability or disability, and any setting.

A Few Things to Consider

- Escalation time is not a teaching time
- This is not a good time for discussion
- Remember how your thinking brain gets turned off when you are escalated? You must remember that the escalated person has a similar mindset.
- When their thinking brain is off, you have to appeal to their survival brain.

Responses and Responsiveness

- Negotiating with an escalated person will likely be unproductive, if they are truly escalated.
- If you are able to negotiate with the person, they are probably not that escalated. their responsiveness is a reflection of their escalation.
- If they cannot make any sense out of what you are doing or saying, that is a sign of their escalation.
- Their response is feedback for you and how you should respond.

5 Surprises

- 1. Manage yourself first before managing others
- 2. One response does not fit all
- 3. Making it stop does not make it stop
- 4. Postvention Prevents Problems
- 5. Inside-Out Change

1. Manage yourself first before managing others

- During an airline safety briefing you are instructed when the mask drops to first place it on yourself before assisting anyone else.
- *Why? You've got to take care of yourself before you can take care of anyone else.*

2. One response does not fit all

- A common misconception of de-escalation skills is that you can learn a specific technique and it will always deescalate the person in front of you.
- It is not uncommon to hear people say, "I usually do _____, but this one time it didn't work."

3. Making it stop does not make it stop

- We have to remember that behavior is a form of communication. It may not always be a good form, but it is a valid form of communication.
- Human nature drives people to get their needs met in whatever ways possible.
- To understand what a person is communicating, we not only have to listen to their words but also "listen" to their behavior and their body language.

3. Making it stop does not make it stop

Two Fundamental Questions:
1) "What is this person trying to gain?"
2) "What is this person trying to avoid?"

4. Postvention Prevents Problems

- **Prevention** is the preparation before an event to ensure it doesn't happen.
- **Postvention** is what you learn after an event that allows you to prevent it from happening again.
- Maybe you were unable to foresee or prevent this incident from happening this time, but what you learn from this incident you can use to prevent it from occurring in the future.

4. Postvention Prevents Problems

- Postvention prevents problems because you can only prevent something from occurring when you can foresee it.
- This means you need to *assess what has already occurred* and decide what should happen next time.
- This is a critical turning point in always having the right response.
- You are most likely to know what to do in an event when you have already planned for it.
- In a long-term approach, this will be your most critical work.

5. Inside Out Change
Changing your way of thinking and responding in order to make a difference in the situation at hand.

- *Inside-Out Change* is a significant de-escalation strategy.
- It comes from within and reflects the change you make regarding the situation.
- Earlier, it was mentioned that the goal of always being in control of a situation.
- It turns out that *if you can change your thinking about a situation, you can change the outcome.*

3 Guiding Principles for Every Situation

- **1 – Meet the needs** of the person that you're dealing with.
- Meet their individual needs, their needs in that moment as well as their long-term needs.

3 Guiding Principles for Every Situation

- **2. Reflect respect and dignity** toward the people you're dealing with.
- No matter what this person is calling you or how they are inconveniencing you, the lack of dignity or respect will not help you productively resolve the situation.

3 Guiding Principles for Every Situation

- 3-It is always the right response to **maintain the safety of everyone** involved.

Summary
5 Surprises
- 1. Manage yourself first before managing others
- 2. One response does not fit all
- 3. Making it stop does not make it stop
- 4. Postvention Prevents Problems
- 5. Inside-Out Change
  - 3 Guiding Principles for Every Situation
- 1. Needs
- 2. Respect
- 3. Safety

Summary

Remain in control always.

Support anyone, anywhere, with any issue

Avoid the wrong response which can make the situation worse.

All Recovery Meeting

End Section One Slides

SECTION TWO

INTRODUCTION TO SECTION TWO

This section contains many aspects of the family system of a family that has a substance use disorder (SUD) or co-occurring disorder (COD) of one or more of its members. We start off with 10 slides that depict a family going from active use to recovery. And then we show the various roles that different family members can take on where there is a SUD/COD within the family. (These are adopted from the work of Sharon Wegscheider-Cruse)

There is also a variety of different family behaviors that are discussed in this section. Most of this is derived from Dr. Murray Bowen's work. He was a Family Therapist that brought new knowledge on family systems that have a SUD/COD issue. We present on such topics as, emotional buttons, co-dependency, enabling and differentiation.

Following are the traits of a healthy family and aspects of family wellness. There is a small section that discusses family sculpting. This allows for the reader to place family members in certain special connection to each other in the form a brief picture of the family as is seen in the present.

The presentation of Section Two is the acknowledgement that it is not just the person who is afflicted with SUD/COD that is affected, but it is the whole family system that is affected.

Peace…… & ……Harmony

TRAINING OBJECTIVES

Module 4
- Roles in a Family with Co-Occurring Issues
- Silently Marginalized

Module 5
- Emotional Buttons
- Differentiation and Un-differentiation
- Codependency
- Enabling

Module 6
- Family Reaction to Recovery
- Traits of a Healthy Family
- Family Sculpting

Module 4

FROM CO-OCCURRING DISORDER (COD) TO RECOVERY

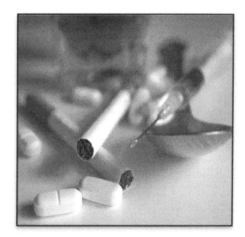

ROLES IN A FAMILY WITH CO-OCCURRING ISSUES

Sharon Wegscheider-Cruse, a family therapist and a nationally known consultant, educator and author, has identified roles that are typically found in family systems with addiction/co-occurring issues.

Six roles have been identified:
- Substance Abuser
- Chief Enabler
- Family Hero
- Family Scapegoat
- Lost Child
- Family Mascot

Some of these roles may be interchangeable in that one person may take on more than one of these roles.

Substance Abuser

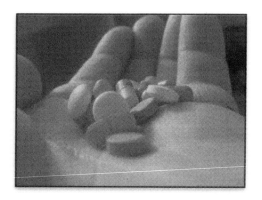

Role:
- To act irresponsibly

Purpose:
- To suppress basic marital conflict and divert attention from more threatening family issues.

Nature of substance abuser:
- Displays emotional detachment
- Abandonment of parental power
- His/her central activity is the drug use and as a result
- Family life diminishes in importance

Chief Enabler

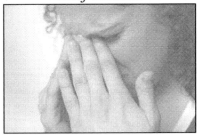

Role:
- To reduce tension in the family by smoothing things over

Purpose:
- To offer the family a sense of stability and protection

Nature of Chief Enabler:
- Is unaware that their enabling behavior is contributing to the progression of the addiction
- Believes they are being helpful and acting to keep the family together

Family Hero

Role:
- To be a source of pride for the family

Purpose:
- To offer the family a sense of being okay; provides hope and something to feel good about

Nature of Family Hero:
- Usually is the oldest child
- Attempts to do everything right
- Helps care for younger siblings and with household chores
- Frequently does well academically and athletically
- Many later become "workaholics"
- May become susceptible to stress-related illnesses later in adulthood
- May be prone to Type A behavior as an adult

Family Scapegoat

Role:
- Alter ego of the Family Hero

Purpose:
- To offer family a sense of purpose by providing someone to blame

Nature of Family Hero:
- Is usually the second oldest child
- Expresses the family's anger and frustration
- Male: may be violent
- Female: may run away or become promiscuous
- BOTH: Most likely to abuse drugs
- Role allows chemically dependent parent to blame someone else for their own drinking/drugging
- Shields the parent from some of the blame and resentment that otherwise would be directed at them

Lost Child

Role:
- Seeks to avoid conflict at all costs

Purpose:
- To offer family a sense of relief and success and is not a source of trouble

Nature of Lost Child:
- May be the youngest or middle child
- Very shy and withdrawn
- Tend to be followers and not leaders
- Often think the family wouldn't notice if they left
- Fears taking risks so may have difficulty with developmental transitions
- May put off making decisions about careers or housing
- May have trouble with intimate relationships
- May exhibit a myriad of mental health problems in adulthood

Family Mascot

Role:
- To play the family clown

Purpose:
- To bring laughter and fun into the family

Nature of Family Mascot:
- Often is the youngest child
- Has a dire need for approval
- Viewed as fragile and vulnerable
- Behaviors serve as defense against feelings of anxiety and inadequacy
- As adults are likeable but appear anxious
- May self-medicate with alcohol or tranquilizers
- May be the one family member that nobody complains about

Exercise: Family Roles Discussion

What are your reactions to the slides?

Do you identify with any of the family roles? If so, how and what?

SILENTLY MARGINALIZED

Family Systems: Gillette and Co-dependency
The diseases of Substance Use Disorder (SUD) and mental illnesses (Co-occurring disorders) bring families down no matter what their socioeconomic status

Even those that can afford the plush, resort-style treatment centers …

Even though the family thinks they are free…
This Luxury Suite is effectively a Prison

Exercise – Family Imprisonment/ Silently Marginalization

Reflect on ways that you feel a family is silently marginalized due to having a member afflicted with a co-occurring disorder

What feelings or emotions do you think can arise?

Module 5

EMOTIONAL BUTTONS

EMOTIONAL BUTTONS DEFINED/IDENTIFIED

Emotional buttons are words or behaviors that can get you upset very quickly. Our loved ones have access to 'emotional buttons' in us that no one else has.

Someone we don't know very well, cannot push our emotional buttons in the way that our children or other family members can.

Dr. Mitch Abblett, a clinical psychologist who specializes in working with troubled youth and their families, presented a set of questions in an article in Psychology Today designed to uncover our emotional buttons.

While considering the following questions, it is important to remember:
"Our buttons are primarily learned patterns: what is learned can be unlearned and need not be permanent."

Exercise: Emotional Buttons

1. How would you describe the overall emotional "volume level" in your house when you were young? What number on a scale of 1 to 10 would you give it, and what words or images come to mind?

2. As a child, what was it like to openly express worries or fear in your family?

3. How was affection shown in your home as a child?

4. How was failure responded to in your family?

5. If others were upset with you when you were young, what would you tend to do? What was it like to be with others when they were upset with you? How would it feel after the interaction? What specific episode comes to mind most readily?

6. When growing up, if you were upset with others, what would you tend to do? How was your experience of vulnerability responded to by others when you were young? What did you learn to do with that experience?

7. List the most challenging emotion (or emotions) for you to experience and openly express when you were growing up. What did you learn about this emotion that made you less than completely comfortable with it? What was the "unwritten rule" about it?

Understanding Your Responses

It may help to continue to journal in response to them over a period of days or weeks. Often, such questioning can lead to difficult memories of the past. This is understandable and is a normal part of the process of change. The effort you put into understanding your patterns of reaction, will INEVITABLY be beneficial to you and your loved ones.

Consider sharing your increased awareness with a spouse, partner or other supportive person in order to help generate more momentum for putting your emotional buttons out of your loved one's "reach."

DIFFERENTIATION AND UNDIFFERENTIATION

Family Systems: Bowen and differentiation
Bowen Family Systems therapists believe that all family dysfunctions, including substance abuse comes from ineffective management of the anxiety in a family system. More specifically, substance abuse is viewed as one way for both individuals and the family as a group to manage anxiety.

The Undifferentiated Self
A huge component of the Bowen Theory is the concept of the 'undifferentiated self' which means being heavily dependent upon the acceptance and approval of others.

People with a poorly "differentiated self" depend heavily on the acceptance and approval of others that they either quickly adjust what they think, say or do to please others *or* they use power/control to coerce others to conform. For example,
- People who either do too much for others (ending up feeling like a victim)
- Bullies/rebels use anger and control (perpetrators, offenders).

Here lies the parallel with co-dependency.

Exercise: The Undifferentiated Self Part 1
Use the space below to journal your thoughts on the undifferentiated self.

Exercise: The Undifferentiated Self Part 2
Less differentiated people and families are more vulnerable to periods of heightened chronic anxiety which contributes to them having a disproportionate share of society's most serious problems. Use the space below to journal your thoughts on this statement.

The Well-Differentiated Self

Bowen's concept of a well-differentiated self is:
- The person has developed an inner acceptance of his own dependence vs. interdependence on others and can stay relatively calm and clear headed in the face of conflict, criticism or rejection, by being responsive rather than *reactive* to situations or people.
- The person is confident in their thinking without polarizing differences.

Exercise: Un-Differentiated and Well-Differentiated

Take a moment and reflect on the concepts offered of "un-differentiated and well-differentiated self. Do you see these concepts manifested in your family system?

Bowen's "Differentiation of Self"

How does this differentiation occur?
- The less developed a person's "self", the more impact others have on his functioning.
- The less differentiated a person is, the more he tries to control, either actively or passively, the functioning of others.
- Relationships during childhood determine how much "self" he develops.
- This rarely changes except with long term effort.
- It is important that for one to reach this stage of a differentiated self, they must be able to separate their own emotional and intellectual activities, from that of the family.
- The need to be aware of how your old story invades into your now/your present is a very important part of the ***differentiated self***.

An example

An eighteen-year-old is leaving home for the first time and taking his/her belief systems (family sacred rules) out into the world.

This person will be controlled by the degree of fusion (his/her loss of a separate self in relationships to others), as to his level of differentiation.

CO-DEPENDENCY

Exercise: Family Restricted

Please reflect on ways that you feel your family is restricted due to having someone in your family afflicted with a substance use disorder. What feelings or emotions arise?

Exercise: Defining Co-Dependency

How would you define Co-dependency?

"The Co-dependent is a spirit divided from itself."

Definition of Co-dependency

Co-dependency is defined as a dysfunctional pattern of living and problem solving which is nurtured by a set of rules within the family system. It is these unwritten family rules (we can also call them Sacred Rules) that affect our approach to living. Each family has their Sacred Rules.

Common Characteristics of Co-dependency

- Difficulty identifying feelings
- Difficulty expressing feelings
- Difficulty forming and maintaining close relationships
- Perfectionism or black and white thinking
- Rigid attitudes and behaviors
- Difficulty adjusting to change
- Feeling overly responsible for the feelings and behaviors of others
- Constant need for approval from others
- Difficulty making decisions
- General feelings of powerlessness over one's life
- A basic sense of shame and low self-esteem over perceived failures in their life

Misconceptions About Co-dependency

Many co-dependent people appear to be very self-sufficient, strong and in control of their lives. Does this sound familiar?

> "Everyone thinks I am so strong, and all of my friends and relatives come to me with their problems, but if they only knew the real me they would be very surprised. Sometimes it's all I can do just to get through each day."

How a Co-dependent Relationship Develops

Co-dependency is a developmental process from early childhood through adulthood

- The co-dependent learns to do only those things which will get him/her the approval and acceptance of others.
- The co-dependent denies much of who he or she really is, with loss of self-identity and self-awareness, because the needs of others are more important than the needs of themselves.

The Development of the Co-dependent Self

At birth, our private self and our public self are equal. Who we appear to be on the outside is who we are on the inside. As we learn to deny who we are and as we try too hard to live up to other's expectations our real self gets stuck and our public self gets distorted. A co-dependent shows up in different roles for different circumstances.

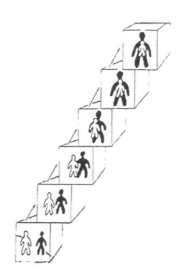

ENABLING

How Do You Define Enabling?
Family Systems Gillette and Bowen Approach: Enabling
Now that you're familiar with some of the roles typically present in the family system, we'll turn our attention back to Gillette and the Bowen approach and focus on the role of the Enabler. Enabling is a term that is widely used in literature in the field of substance use/co-occurring disorders.

Exercise: Definition of Enabling
How would you define enabling? Take a few moments to form your definition.
Within your group, discuss enabling and develop a working definition. Write down your definition. Be prepared to report out to the larger group.

Your Definition

Group Definition

Definition of Enabling

In a SUD or Co-occurring family system the word **Enabler** defines the behaviors of the **Co-dependent**.

The **Enabler** is an individual who reacts to the symptoms of the illness (disease of addiction) in such a way as to <u>shield the dependent</u> person from experiencing the full impact of the harmful consequences of the disease. The greater the <u>enabling</u>, the greater the <u>fusion</u> (loss of a separate self in relationship to others) of that individual.

Correlation between the Enabler and the Dual-diagnosed Person

The disease affects the *dependent* in bad behaviors, violation of the individual's internal value system and growing feelings of guilt remorse and shame.

The disease affects the *enabler* by excusing the behavior of the chemically dependent. Self-worth becomes tied to the dependent person (fusion) and there are growing feelings of guilt, embarrassment and anger. A lot of times, enabling just seems like it is the right thing to do.

Progression of Enabling

<u>Stage One: Protection</u>

The enabler performs small tasks for the dependent such as calling in sick, picking up after them, or seeing they get to appointments.

4 Defenses used by the dependent	**Enabler's Response**
Rationalization:	Believes it
Repression:	Feels "Crazy"
Projections:	Says "it's my fault"
Irresponsible:	Over-responsible

<u>Stage Two: Controlling</u>

The enabler takes over larger responsibilities, such as the handling of financial matters, supplying room and board for a young adult, or trying to control the dependent's chemical use.

<u>Stage Three: Super People or Martyr</u>

The enabler begins to receive increasing positive feedback for "hanging in there" or "going the extra mile". At this stage, the enabler has grown so accustomed to their role that new found sobriety for the chemical dependent creates a traumatic emotional upheaval.

Why People Enable

- Delusion about the situation and are unaware of enabling.
- Feelings of apathy, tiredness and inadequacy which may keep one from trying any new approach to the problem.
- Feel a need to protect the dependent and themselves.
- Get good feelings for being responsible.
- Like being in control and may enjoy the position of power held.
- Receive praise from society.
- Like the role of being a martyr.

Personal Definition

The following is a quote about being enabled from the authors of the program, who are now in long term recovery:

> "At the time, we were able to instantly pick up on when the person was enabling us and that they were thinking, it is the right thing to do. It was then an easy task to take advantage of that. As long as there was an enabler looking out for me, it gave me permission to continue my use and abuse. It wasn't until my enabler started to communicate to me their feelings and needs directly and set up boundaries, that I was forced to look at myself. This did not change me right away, but after a while, I had to face the facts. I didn't have the cover up that comes from the enabler. I was uncovered without protection and cover-ups. Fortunately for us, we started into recovery".

Three C's about Chemical Dependency and Co-occurring Disorders

- You didn't **cause** the disease.
- You can't **control** the disease.
- You can't **cure** the disease

Module 6
RECOVERY – HEALTHY FAMILY

From Co-Dependency to Interdependency
Process of moving out of "unhealthy" co-dependency and into "healthy" interdependency

In order to move successfully from co-dependency to interdependency, a person must rise above family emotionality (family drama) and develop a <u>loyalty to self</u> that is not dominated by covert loyalties to <u>previous generations</u>. In addition, a person must gain a clear, clean title to his own <u>destiny</u>, unencumbered by debts or events of the past.

This goes back to the need to be responsible for self as an important factor in being a Recovery Family Mentor.

Healthy Interdependency
Healthy interdependency consists of partners who go out of their way for each other; they are *interdependent*. Only relatively healthy people are capable of interdependent relationships, which involve give and take. It is not unhealthy to unilaterally give during a time when your partner is having difficulty. You know your partner will reciprocate should the tables turn.

However, ...
> "Interdependency also implies that you do not have to give until it hurts. By comparison, in a co-dependent relationship, one partner does almost all the giving, while the other does almost all the taking, *almost all the time*." – Dr. Irene Matiatos

To Recovery and a Healthy Family
"Family members who are impacted by mental illness, alcohol, gambling and other drug problems have been long cursed by social stigma, public neglect, and professional misunderstanding. Parents, spouses and children of the addicted have hidden most life-shaping experiences behind a veil of silence and secrecy. Throughout the history of addiction in the U.S., family members have been castigated more as causative agents and sources of recovery sabotage than as recovery resources or individuals deserving services in their own right".

Let's overcome this stigma……………………………….

White, W., & Savage, B. (2005). All in the family: Alcohol and other drug problems, recovery, advocacy. *Alcoholism Treatment Quarterly, 23(4), 3-37.*

A Happy Family in Recovery

The Long Road out of Co-dependency into Recovery

Addiction has been characterized as a genetic, social, psychological and spiritual disorder. The Bowen Family Systems Theory perspective, describes it as an aspect of a multi-generational emotional process.

New-found recovery can stress (chronic anxiety) the family by disrupting patterns of interacting, until new roles are generated. The newly recovered Alcoholic/Addict begins practicing new behaviors which throws the family into chaos when their behaviors, that have been the norm in dealing with the Alcoholic/Addict, no longer work.

Family Responses to a Co-occurring Disordered Person Clean and Well

- A family member can replace the addicted person's role by becoming the family's acting out co-occurring person. This immediately resolves the crisis, as family members can maintain their old roles and live by the old rules.
- The family may dissolve into many parts. The other parent may divorce the recovering parent.
- The family might have had so much pain recently, that they are willing to go to great lengths to get some relief. <u>Meaning that the family may reach out for support and recovery as a unit.</u>
- The family may undertake the deep work and commitment that is required to develop a whole new set of family rules.

Exercise: Family Response to Recovery

Split up into dyads and discuss how a family may react (what they may do) when a family member begins their journey to recovery.

How to Support a Newly Recovering Family

- Stress "Self-focus" for individual family members. The beginning process requires each person to get as healthy as possible.
- Keep system as calm as possible. Encourage family members to focus on getting support for themselves.
- Help them set small, practical, manageable goals for the family during initial crisis.
- Make referrals, when possible, that treat the entire family.
- Address lack of trust and fear of relapse.
- Begin to teach new coping skills to deal with the changes

One of these new skills for coping is detachment.

What is Detachment?

DETACHMENT – is neither kind nor unkind. It does not imply judgment or condemnation of the person or situation from which we are detaching. Separating ourselves from the adverse effects of another person's Co-occurring Disorder can be a means of detaching: this does not necessarily require physical separation. Detachment can help us look at our situations realistically and objectively.

DETACHMENT – Allows us to let go of our obsession with another's behavior and begin to lead happier and more manageable lives. It allows us lives with dignity and rights, lives guided by a Power greater than ourselves. We can still love the person without liking the behavior. (*adopted from the AL-Anon Family Group brochure on Detachment*)

Traits of a Healthy Family

The following was adopted and modified from Dolores Curran's "Traits of a Healthy Family."

- The healthy family communicates and listens, supports and affirms one another.
- The healthy family teaches respect for others and develops a sense of trust.
- It enjoys a sense of play and humor, and exhibits a sense of shared responsibility.
- The healthy family teaches a strong sense of right and wrong and has a strong sense of family in which tradition abound.
- It has a healthy balance of interaction among family members.
- The healthy family has a shared spirituality core, and respects the privacy of one another.
- It shares leisure and meal times.

And very importantly…
the healthy family admits to and seeks help for problems.

Exercise – Traits of a Healthy Family

Select the from the traits listed above, those that you can incorporate into your family now. After 5 minutes, we will discuss this as a group.

Remember:
We have looked at:
- Healthy ways and what outcomes are possible when you move from co-dependency to interdependency.
- The road from co-dependency to recovery.

This implies that if you are a friend or family member that has been affected by the dual-diagnosed, you need to understand that you are a family member also in recovery. Understanding this will go a long way in improving your effectiveness as a helper. It is important to remember as the dual-diagnosed person is recovering, so must the family be recovering.

FAMILY SCULPTING

Definition of Family Sculpting

"Family sculpting essentially involves the family in the formation of a 'living sculpture' as directed by one of the members-the sculptor-under the general direction of the therapist." (Jeff Hearn and Marilyn Lawrence, 2003)

Family Sculpting

- In a family group therapy setting, a family member may be asked to place other family members in relation to other family members.
- Perhaps the parents will be placed in the center, but not so close together.
- Perhaps the siblings will be placed in a close group, with one sibling placed far from the others, but close to one of the parents.
- Then the family members who were placed in their positions may be asked about their perception of this placement.
- The member who performed the family sculpture may be asked how the family system would be different in five years, if the relationships and behaviors continue as they are. Then another family member does a family sculpture and the process is repeated.

As shown in the illustration below, the mother and daughter appear to have a strong, loving bond. The father and son appear to be alienated not only from the family, but from each other as well.

As shown in the illustration below, the parents appear to be a unit, but the daughter appears to be closer to the father. The son appears to be emotionally cut off from the family, and no one seems to enjoy the bond depicted of the mother and daughter in the first example.

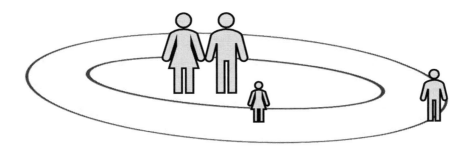

Here is an example of a family that is dysfunctional. You can tell by the various statement that are made that there is no cohesiveness.

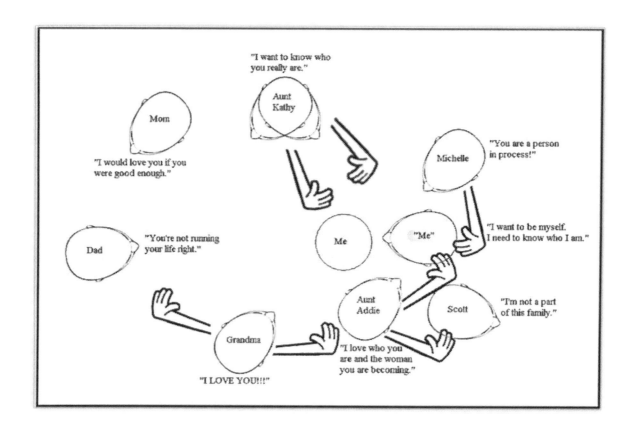

Exercise – Your Family Sculpture

In the space below, draw a sample of your family sculpture. Be prepared to present your family sculpture to the group. You may involve as many participants that you feel may be necessary.

SECTION TWO SLIDES

Behavioral Health Mentor Training

Day 2

Trainers: Richard D Dávila, Ph.D.
Jackie Sue Griffin, MBA, MS

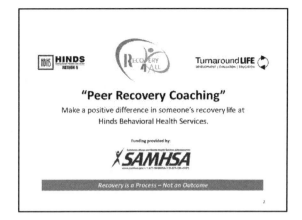

"Peer Recovery Coaching"
Make a positive difference in someone's recovery life at Hinds Behavioral Health Services.

Today's Agenda

- Roles in a Family
- Silently Marginalized
- Emotional Buttons
- Differentiation and Un-differentiation
- Codependency
- Enabling

Today's Agenda

- Family Reaction to Recovery
- Traits of a Healthy Family
- Family Sculpting
- *All Recovery Meeting*

Co-occurring Disorders to Recovery

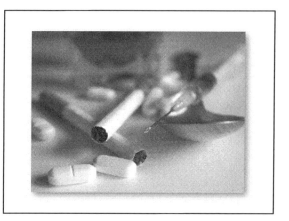

The Family

Roles in a Family

Sharon Wegscheider-Cruse: Backround

- Family Therapist
- Nationally known consultant, educator and Author
- Founding Chairperson of the National Association for children of Alcoholics (NACOA)
- Chairs countless conferences and conventions and provides keynote presentations

Typical Roles

- Substance Abuser
- Chief Enabler
- Family Hero
- Family Scapegoat
- Lost Child
- Family Mascot

Substance Abuser

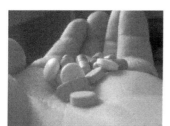

Substance Abuser Role and Purpose

- Role
  - To act irresponsibly
- Purpose
  - To suppress basic marital conflict and divert attention from more threatening family issues

Nature of Substance Abuser

- Displays emotional detachment
- Abandonment of parental power
- His/her central activity is the drug use and as a result
- Family life diminishes in importance

Chief Enabler

Chief Enabler Role and Purpose

- Role
  - To reduce tension in the family by smoothing things over
- Purpose
  - Offers the family a sense of stability and protection

Nature of Chief Enabler

- Is unaware that their enabling behavior is contributing to the progression of the addiction
- Believe they are being helpful and acting to keep the family together

Family Hero

Family Hero Role and Purpose

- Role
  - To be a source of pride for the family
- Purpose
  - Offers the family a sense of being okay
  - Provides hope and something to feel good about

Nature of Family Hero

- Usually is the oldest child
- Attempts to do everything right
- Helps care for younger siblings and with household chores
- Frequently does well academically and athletically

Nature of Family Hero

- Many later become "workaholics"
- May become susceptible to stress-related illnesses later in adulthood
- May be prone to Type A behavior as an adult

Family Scapegoat

Family Scapegoat Role and Purpose

- Role
  - Alter ego of the Family Hero
- Purpose
  - Offers family a sense of purpose by providing someone to blame

Nature of Family Scapegoat

- Usually is the second oldest child
- Expresses the family's anger and frustration
- Male: may be violent
- Female: may run away or become promiscuous
- BOTH: Most likely to abuse drugs

Nature of Family Scapegoat

- Role allows chemically dependent parent to blame someone else for their own drinking/drugging
- Shields the parent from some of the blame and resentment that otherwise would be directed at them

Lost Child

Lost Child Role and Purpose

- Role
  - Seeks to avoid conflict at all costs
- Purpose
  - Offers family a sense of relief and success and is not a source of trouble

Nature of Lost Child

- May be the youngest or middle child
- Very shy and withdrawn
- Tend to be followers and not leaders
- Often think the family wouldn't notice if they left
- Fears taking risks so may have difficulty with developmental transitions (put off making decisions)

Nature of Lost Child

- May put off making decisions about careers or housing
- May have trouble with intimate relationships
- May exhibit a myriad of mental health problems in adulthood

Family Mascot

Family Mascot Role and Purpose

- Role
  - To play the family clown
- Purpose
  - To bring laughter and fun into the family

Nature of Family Mascot

- Is often the youngest child
- Has a dire need for approval
- Viewed as fragile and vulnerable
- Behaviors serve as defense against feelings of anxiety and inadequacy
- As adults are likeable but appear anxious
- May self-medicate with alcohol or tranquilizers
- May be the one family member that nobody complains about

Exercise: Family Roles and You

Silently Marginalized

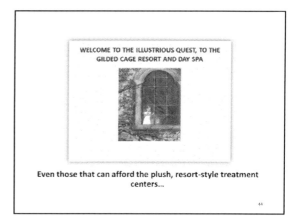

Even those that can afford the plush, resort-style treatment centers...

Even though the family thinks they are free...

The family is effectively silently marginalized

How is A Family Silently Marginalized?

Emotional Buttons

Emotional Buttons

Words or behaviors that can get you upset very quickly

Our loved ones have access to these "emotional buttons" in us that no one else has

Dr. Mitch Abblett on Emotional Buttons:

"Understanding will be the first step, but will be insufficient by itself.

The real work will be in committing to practice interrupting these reactions and inserting new, more helpful responses to your loved ones' behavior."

Exercise: Uncovering Your Emotional Buttons

"By reviewing and deeply considering the questions in this exercise, you will have a greater understanding of your emotional buttons.

"While considering these questions, it is important to remember:

"Our buttons are primarily learned patterns; what is learned can be unlearned and need not be permanent."

Understanding Your Responses

Often, such questioning can lead to difficult memories of the past. This is understandable and a normal part of the process of change.

Understanding your patterns of reaction will INEVITABLY be beneficial to you and your loved ones.

Which Is More Important?

Reacting negatively and intensely to button-pushing (and maybe feeling as though your were "right" or "made your point")

OR

NOT reacting (and maybe feel as though you "lost" in the moment) in order to take leadership of bad situations and model how to manage difficulty?

The Undifferentiated Self

Bowen's "Undifferentiated Self"

People with a poorly "differentiated self"

- depend so heavily on the acceptance and approval of others that they either quickly adjust what they think, say or do to please others or they use power/control to coerce others to conform.

For example:

people who either do too much for others (ending up feeling like a victim)

or

bullies/rebels who use anger and control (perpetrators, offenders).

Here lies the parallel with co-dependency.

Bowen's "Undifferentiated Self"

Less differentiated people and families are more vulnerable to periods of heightened chronic anxiety which contributes to them having a disproportionate share of society's most serious problems.

The Well-Differentiated Self

Bowen's Concept of a Well-differentiated "Self"

- The person has developed an inner acceptance of his own dependence vs. interdependence on others and can stay relatively calm and clear headed in the face of conflict, criticism or rejection, by being *responsive* rather than *reactive* to situations or people.
- This person is confident in their thinking without polarizing differences.

How Does Differentiation Occur?

Bowen's "Differentiation of Self"

- The less developed a person's "self", the more impact others have on his functioning.
- The less differentiated a person is, the more he tries to control, either actively or passively, the functioning of others.
- Relationships during childhood determine how much "self" he develops.
- This rarely changes except with long term effort.

Bowen's "Differentiation of Self"

- It is important that for one to reach this stage, they must be able to separate their own emotional and intellectual activities, from that of the family.
- The need to be aware of how your old story invades into your now/your present is a very important part of the *differentiated self*.

An Example

- We will begin to see an eighteen year old, leaving home for the first time and taking their belief systems (family sacred rules) out into the world.
- This person will be controlled by the degree of fusion (his loss of a separate self in relationships to others), as to his level of differentiation.

Substance Abuse, Co-Dependency and Family Systems

The Bowen System
and the
Alcoholic/Addict Family

by Russell Gillette, LPC, LADC

Co-dependency

Co-dependency

"The Co-dependent is a spirit divided from itself."

Definition of Co-dependency

- Co-dependency is defined as a dysfunctional pattern of living and problem solving which is nurtured by a set of rules within the family system.
- It is these unwritten family rules (we can also call them Sacred Rules) that affect our approach to living. Each family has their Sacred Rules.

Common Characteristics of Co-Dependency

- Difficulty identifying feelings
- Difficulty expressing feelings
- Difficulty forming and maintaining close relationships
- Perfectionism or black and white thinking
- Rigid attitudes and behaviors
- Difficulty adjusting to change

Common Characteristics of Co-Dependency

- Feeling overly responsible for the feelings and behaviors of others
- Constant need for approval from others
- Difficulty making decisions
- General feelings of powerlessness over one's life
- A basic sense of shame and low self-esteem over perceived failures in their life

Co-dependency and its Origins

- Originally thought to only affect individuals directly involved with a chemically or COD dependent person.
- Initially considered to be an unhealthy pattern of coping with life, as a reaction to someone else's alcohol, drug or COD.

Misconceptions About Co-dependency

Misconceptions about Co-dependency

- Many co-dependent people appear to be very self-sufficient, "Strong" and in control of their lives.
- Example: "Everyone thinks I am so strong, and all of my friends and relatives come to me with their problems, but if they only knew the real me they would be very surprised. Sometimes it's all I can do just to get through each day."

Co-dependent Rules

- These rules have to do with protecting or isolating oneself from others by not taking risks to get close.
- People who have grown up with these rules don't realize that there are many families that:
    - do allow an individual to talk about problems within or outside the family,
    - to express emotions openly,
    - to make mistakes without undue criticism and being vulnerable and asking for help is both routine and okay.

How do we get to this point?

- The co-dependent learns to do only those things which will get him/her the approval and acceptance of others.
- The co-dependent denies much of who he or she really is, with loss of self-identity and self-awareness, because the needs of others are more important than the needs of himself or herself.

The Development of the Co-dependent Self

At birth our private self and our public self are equal. Who we appear to be on the outside is who we are on the inside.

As we learn to deny who we are and as we try too hard to live up to other's expectations, our real self gets stuck and our public self gets distorted.

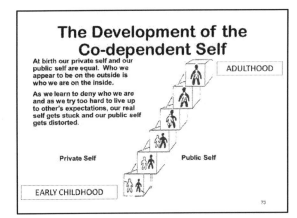

Private Self   Public Self

EARLY CHILDHOOD — ADULTHOOD

Family Systems
Gillette and Bowen Approach: Enabling

How Do You Define Enabling?

- How would you define enabling? Take a few moments to form your own definition.
- Within your group, discuss enabling and develop a working definition. Write down your definition. Be prepared to report out to the larger group.

ENABLING

- In an SUD or Co-occurring family system the word *Enabler* defines the behaviors of the *Co-dependent*.
- The *Enabler* is an individual who reacts to the symptoms of the illness (disease of addiction) in such a way as to shield the dependent person from experiencing the full impact of the harmful consequences of the disease.
- The greater the enabling, the greater the fusion (loss of a separate self in relationship to others) of that individual.

Correlation between the Enabler and the Dual-Diagnosed Person

- How the Disease affects the Dependent
  - Destructive Behaviors
  - Internal Value system is violated
  - Growing feelings of guilt, remorse and shame

Correlation between the Enabler and the Dual-Diagnosed Person

- How the Disease affects the Enabler
  - Excuses behavior of the chemically dependent
  - Self-worth becomes tied to the Dependent person (Fusion)
  - Growing feelings of guilt, embarrassment and anger

Progression of Enabling

Stage One – **Protection**.
- Small tasks are done for the dependent such as calling in sick, picking up after them, or seeing they get to appointments.

4 Defenses used by the dependent	Enabler's Response
Rationalization	Believes it
Repression	Feels "Crazy"
Projections	Says "it's my fault"
Irresponsible	Over-responsible

Progression of Enabling

Stage Two – **Controlling**.
- Larger responsibilities are taken over, such as:
  - handling of financial matters
  - supplying room and board for a young adult
  - trying to control the dependent's chemical use

Progression of Enabling

Stage Three – **Super People or Martyr.**
- Begins to receive increasing positive feedback for "hanging in there" or "going the extra mile".
- At this stage, the enabler has grown so accustomed to their role that new found sobriety for the chemical dependent part of COD creates a traumatic emotional upheaval.

Why People Enable

- Deluded about the situation
  Not aware of their enabling (think they're doing the "right" thing).
- Feelings of apathy, tiredness and inadequacy
  These feelings keep them from trying new approaches to the problem.

Why People Enable

- Feelings of Fear
  They are scared for the dependent and feel a need to protect the dependent and themselves.
- They get good feelings for being responsible
  Like being in control, and for some, actually enjoying the position of power that they have.
  Enablers also receive praise from our society.

Personal Definition

The following is a quote about being enabled from the authors of the program, who are now in long term recovery:

"At the time, we were able to instantly pick up on when the person was enabling us and that they were thinking, it is the right thing to do. It was then an easy task to take advantage of that. As long as there was an enabler looking out for me, it gave me permission to continue my use and abuse. It wasn't until my enabler started to communicate to me their feelings and needs directly and set up boundaries, that I was forced to look at myself. This did not change me right away, but after a while, I had to face the facts. I didn't have the cover up that comes from the enabler. I was uncovered without protection and cover-ups. Fortunately for us, we started into recovery".

Three C's about Chemical Dependency and Co-occurring

Enablers need to learn:
- You didn't **cause** the disease.
- You can't **control** the disease.
- You can't **cure** the disease.

Family Reaction to Recovery

The Long Road out of Co-dependency into Recovery

Addiction has been characterized as a genetic, social, psychological and spiritual disorder. The Bowen Family Systems Theory perspective, describes it as an aspect of a multi-generational emotional process.

The Long Road out of Co-dependency into Recovery

New-found recovery can stress (chronic anxiety) the family by disrupting patterns of interacting, until new roles are generated. The newly recovered person begins practicing new behaviors which throws the family into chaos when their behaviors, that have been the norm in dealing with the recoveree, no longer work.

Family Responses to a Co-occurring Disordered Person Clean and Well

- A family member can replace the addicted person's role by becoming the family's acting out co-occurring person. This immediately resolves the crisis, as family members can maintain their old roles and live by the old rules.
- The family may dissolve into many parts. The other parent may divorce the recovering parent.

Family Responses to a Co-occurring Disordered Person Clean and Well

- The family might have had so much pain recently, that they are willing to go to great lengths to get some relief. <u>Meaning that the family may reach out for support and recovery as a unit.</u>
- The family may undertake the deep work and commitment that is required to develop a whole new set of family rules.

Exercise: Family Response to Recovery

Split up into dyads and discuss how a family may react (what they may do) when a family member begins their journey to recovery.

How to Support a Newly Recovering Family

- Stress "Self-focus" for individual family members. The beginning process requires each person to get as healthy as possible.
- Keep system as calm as possible. Focus on getting support for themselves.
- Make small, practical, manageable goals for the family during initial crisis.

How to Support a Newly Recovering Family

- Make referrals, when possible, that treat the entire family.
- Address lack of trust and fear of relapse.
- Begin to teach new coping skills to deal with changes

What is Detachment?

DETACHMENT – is neither kind nor unkind. It does not imply judgment or condemnation of the person or situation from which we are detaching. Separating ourselves from the adverse effects of another person's Co-occurring Disorder can be a means of detaching: this does not necessarily require physical separation. Detachment can help us look at our situations realistically and objectively.

What is Detachment?

DETACHMENT – Allows us to let go of our obsession with another's behavior and begin to lead happier and more manageable lives, lives with dignity and rights, lives guided by a Power greater than ourselves. We can still love the person without liking the behavior.

(adopted from the AL-Anon Family Group brochure on Detachment)

Traits of a Healthy Family

Adopted and modified from Dolores Curran's "Traits Of A Healthy Family."

Traits of a Healthy Family

The healthy family:
- communicates and listens.
- affirms & supports one another.
- teaches respect for others.
- develops a sense of trust.
- has a sense of play and humor.
- exhibits a sense of shared responsibility.
- teaches a sense of right and wrong.
- has a strong sense of family in which rituals and tradition abound.

Traits of a Healthy Family

The healthy family:
- has a healthy balance of interaction among family members.
- has a shared spirituality core.
- respects the privacy of one another.
- shares leisure and meal time.

AND VERY IMPORTANTLY ...
The healthy family admits to and seeks help for problems.

Exercise: Traits of a Healthy Family

Select some traits of a healthy family that may need to be incorporated into your family now

After 5 minutes, we will discuss this as a group.

Remember ...

- If you are a friend or a family member that has been affected by the dual-diagnosed person, you need to understand that you are a family member also in recovery.
- Understanding this will go a long way in improving your effectiveness as a helper.
- It is important to remember as the dual-diagnosed person is recovering, so must the family be recovering.

Family Sculpting

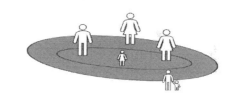

Family Roles

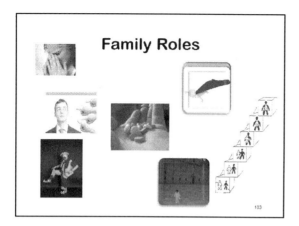

What is Family Sculpting?

- "Family sculpting essentially involves the family in the formation of a 'living sculpture' as directed by one of the members – the sculptor – under the general direction of the therapist"

    (Jeff Hearn and Marilyn Lawrence, 2003)

Family Sculpting – How?

- In a family group therapy setting, a family member may be asked to place other family members in relation to other family members.
    - Perhaps the parents will be placed in the center, but not so close together,
    - Perhaps the siblings will be placed in a close group, with one sibling placed far from the others, but close to one of the parents.

Family Sculpting – How?

- Then the family members who were placed in their positions may be asked about their perception of this placement.
- The member who performed the family sculpture may be asked how the family system would be different in five years, if the relationships and behaviors continues as they are.
- Then another family member does a family sculpture and the process is repeated.

Example of Family Sculpting

Example of Family Sculpting

Another Family Sculpting Example (Dysfunctional)

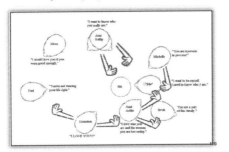

Family Sculpture Demo

Exercise – Your Family Sculpture

All Recovery Meeting

End Section Two Slides

SECTION THREE

INTRODUCTION TO SECTION THREE

This section gets into the importance of ethics in being a Peer Support Specialist. We also present material on Fragility as presented by William White. This is a period of post-acute care where the SUD/COD person is discharged from this phase of treatment and returns to the community in an unstructured environment. He argues that is the period where it is vital that there be recovery support services available like Peer Support Specialist and other supports.

We go on and present the important subject of cultural competency and differentiation in power relationships, such as boss/worker, male/female, poor/middleclass, parent/child, teacher/student, etc. We also present an excerpt from the national Substance Abuse and Mental Health Services Administration (SAMHSA) on medication management.

We end this section with an excerpt from book, "Living Your Life Not Your Story" authored by Dr. Davila and Dr. Secor. Here we discuss the importance to start practicing bringing consciousness into the present, the moment. To many times our story of the past is permitted to enter into our present-day life many times having a negative outcome. We then present issues related to self-care. Helpers need Help. If you are working to help someone else, we should also be attending to our own self-care. This section ends with a presentation of a "Recovery Wellness Plan" where we present 8 areas of building a recovery foundation.

These three sections are a three-day training that leads to much personal and professional growth – which we hope you receive this in reading this workbook.

Peace………… & ………. Serenity

TRAINING OBJTECTIVES

Module 7
- Ethics
- Fragility

Module 8
- Defining Cultural and Cultural Competence
- Power Shuffle
- Medication Management

Module 9
- Live Your Life Not Your Story
- Self-Care
- Recovery Wellness Plan

Module 7
__ETHICS__

What Are Ethics?
Before we can talk about the role ethics play in Peer Support, we need to know what they are. We know we have them. But what are they, or how would you define them.

My personal definition is:

Ethics – A Definition

According to Merriam Webster ...
Ethics are rules of behavior based on ideas about what is morally good and bad.

For RC and CPSS, ethics are:
- A set of developed and accepted standards or principles of behaviors and actions for both individuals and organizations within a profession.
- A standard code of behavior that is created to enhance service provision and create a climate of dignity and respect
- An agreed upon set of morals, values and conduct standards accepted by the group

Exercise: Principle, Morals, Values
Write a simple definition for each of these terms:

Principle

Morals

Values

Some Common Definitions

Principles: – Fundamental truths, laws, doctrine, or motivating forces upon which others are based; a rule of conduct. e.g. Above all, do no harm.

Morals: Principles with respect to right or wrong in conduct.

Values: Social principles, goals, or standards held by an individual, group or society.

Fiduciary – is a term describing relationships in which one person has assumed a special duty and obligation for the care of another.
- The relationship of coach/mentor to recoveree is not one of equal power
- It is a relationship where one party has a higher degree of vulnerability
- Therefore, there is a higher level of obligation than in fully reciprocal relationships

Boundary Management – encompasses the decisions that increase or decrease intimacy within a relationship.
- In more professional relationships, the hierarchical boundaries are more pronounced and are governed by maintaining detachment and distance
- Peer-based recovery support services rely on reciprocity and minimizing social distance
- While both services affirm boundaries of inappropriateness, these boundaries may differ

Multi Party Vulnerability – is a phrase that conveys how multiple parties can be injured by what a RC/CPSS does or fails to do.
- This may include the recoveree, family members, organizations, the larger community of support services, the recovery community and the community at large.

Ethics in Recovery Coaching and Peer Support Specialist Mentoring

A Recovery Coach/ Peer Support Specialist is anyone interested in promoting recovery by removing barriers and obstacles to recovery by serving as a personal guide and mentor for people seeking or in recovery.
- Motivator and Cheerleader
- Ally and Confidant
- Truth Teller
- Role Model and Mentor
- Problem Solver
- Resource Broker
- Advocate
- Community Organizer
- Friend and Companion
- Lifestyle Consultant

Stay in Your Lane

Sponsor
You are moving beyond your role of a Recovery Coach/ Peer Advocate/Peer Support Specialist if you:
- Perform AA/NA or other mutual aid group service work in your role
- Guide someone through the steps or principals of a particular recovery program

Counselor
You are moving beyond your role of a Recovery Coach/Peer Advocate/Peer Support Specialist if you:
- Diagnose
- Provide counseling or refer to your support activities as "counseling" or "therapy"
- Focus on problems/"issues"/trauma as opposed to recovery solutions

Nurse/Doctor
You are moving beyond your role of a Recovery Coach/Peer Advocate/Peer Support Specialist if you:
- Suggest or express disagreement with medical diagnoses (including psychiatric diagnoses)
- Offer medical advice
- Make statements about prescribed drugs

Clergy Person
You are moving beyond your role of a Recovery Coach/Peer Advocate/Peer Support Specialist if you:
- Promote a particular church or religion
- Interpret religious doctrine
- Offer absolution or forgiveness (other than forgiveness for harm done specifically to you)
- Provide pastoral counseling

Exercise: Boundaries

Recovery Coach/Peer Advocate/Peer Support Specialist Theater

In your small groups come up with a scenario that showcases a boundary or ethical issue. Each person in your group must have a role, even if it is not a speaking role.

You have 15 minutes to prepare.

Core Recovery Values and Ethical Conduct

Gratitude and Service
- Carry hope to individuals, families and communities.

Recovery
- All service hinges on personal recovery.

Use of self
- Know thyself; Be the face of recovery; Tell your story; Know when to use your story.

Capability
- Improve yourself; give your best.

Honesty
- Tell the truth; Separate fact from opinion; When wrong, admit it.

Authenticity of Voice
- Accurately represent your recovery experience and the role from which you are speaking

Credibility
- Walk what you talk.

Fidelity
- Keep your promises.

Humility
- Work within the limitations of your experience and role.

Loyalty
- Don't give up; offer multiple chances.

Hope
- Offer self and others as living proof; Focus on the positive – strengths, assets, and possibilities rather than problems and pathology.

Dignity and Respect
- Express compassion; Accept imperfection; Honor each other's potential.

Acceptance
- "The roads to recovery are many" (Wilson, 1944); Learn about diverse pathways and styles of recovery.

Autonomy and Choice
- Recovery is voluntary; It must be chosen; Enhance choices and choice making.

Discretion
- Respect privacy; Don't gossip.

Protection
- Do no harm; Do not exploit; Protect others; Avoid conflicts of interest.

Advocacy
- Challenge injustice; Be a voice for the voiceless; Empower others to speak.

Stewardship
- Use resources wisely.

REMEMBER

To Always Stay in Your Lane
Always, when in Doubt, Check with your Supervisor

FRAGILITY

**Recovery Management and
Recovery-oriented Systems of Care:
Scientific Rationale and Promising Practices
William L. White, MA
Senior Research Consultant
Chestnut Health Systems
2008**

FRAGILITY OF POST-TREATMENT RECOVERY

Individuals leaving addiction treatment are fragilely balanced between recovery and re-addiction in the hours, days, weeks, months, and years following discharge.

These individuals are making recovery and re-addiction decisions during a time in which treatment specialists have disengaged from their lives, but many sources of recovery sabotage are present.

To state that early posttreatment recovery is fragile is not to say that long-term recovery is not possible.

The recovery prevalence rate for persons meeting lifetime criteria for substance use disorders ranges between50-60%. Fifty percent of AA members surveyed report six or more years of recovery, and
51% of people self-identified as "in recovery" in the larger community also report recovery duration of six or more years.

Factors related to post-treatment relapse of adults and adolescents include craving, interpersonal conflict, emotional distress, social pressure to use from peers, exposure to alcohol-/drug-using environments, initial use of a drug other than drug of choice, and a lessening in vigilance and recovery maintenance activities.

Relapse is often embedded in the social interactions that occur after treatment support is withdrawn. There are two dimensions to such interactions:
- contact and communication with active users
- and contact and communication with non-addicts.

The risk of relapse is high when the former offers a siren call to return to a world where so many of the addict's prior needs were met, and the latter includes expressions of hostility, skepticism, and distrust

A meta-analysis of opiate treatment outcome research found post-treatment relapse associated with high levels of pre-treatment drug use, prior treatment, the lack of a prior period of abstinence,
abstinence from alcohol, depression, high levels of stress, unemployment, association with drug using
peers, shorter length of treatment, and leaving treatment prior to completion. Alcohol often plays a role in post-treatment relapse, regardless of drug of choice prior to treatment entry.

Module 8
CULTURE AND CULTURAL COMPETENCE

Exercise: Culture & Cultural Competence Definitions

In your small groups come up with definitions for both Culture and Cultural Competence. *Challenge yourself to do so with a complete sentence and without the use of bullets.*

Culture:

Cultural Competence

Definition of Culture

Culture generally refers to "shared values, norms, traditions, customs, art, history, folklore and institutions of a group of people." (Orlandi, Weston, & Epstein, 1992)

Definition of Cultural Competence

A set of behaviors, attitudes and policies
- that come together in a system, agency, or
- program or among individuals, enabling
- them to function effectively in diverse
- cultural interactions and similarities within,
- among, and between groups."

U.S. Department of Health and Human Services

Cultural Competence is a point on a continuum that represents the *POLICIES and PRACTICES of an organization,* or the VALUES and BEHAVIOR of an *individual* which enable that organization or person to interact effectively in a culturally diverse environment.

POWER SHUFFLE

People experience power and privilege and the lack thereof in numerous ways. The vast majority of us at some point in our lives have found ourselves in a power group and a non-power group.

You are a woman	You have a visible or hidden disability or impairment
You are African-American, Afro-Caribbean, or black or of African descent	Your parents were considered unskilled labor
You are Asian, East-Asian/Indian or Pacific Islander	You or anyone in your family is other than heterosexual
You are Latino/a or Chicano/a	You identify as part of the LGBTQ community,
You are of Arab descent	You were ever called or consider yourself fat
You are Native American or part Native American	You have ever been dangerously or continually sick
You are of Jewish heritage	Your native language is other than English
You were raised poor	You came from a family where alcohol and/or drugs are or were a problem
You were non-degreed	You are a non-management worker and do not supervise anyone on your job
Your parents had no college education	You have ever been unemployed, not by choice
You were raised in ore live in an isolated community or farming community	Are a veteran
You were raised in or presently live in the inner city	You or a member of your family has ever been incarcerated or been in the juvenile justice system
You or your parents are first generation Americans	Under 30
You are other than Christian	Over 60
You or anyone in your family has ever been treated for mental illness	Raised by a single parent
	Are a single parent

MEDICATION MANAGEMENT

What is MedTEAM?

MedTEAM is a systematic, evidence-based approach for offering medication management to people with mental illnesses. It helps those who prescribe medications to integrate the best current research evidence, clinical expertise, and consumer experience

Practice Principles of MedTEAM

- The latest scientific evidence guides medication decisions
- Medication management requires a team approach
- Systematically assessing medication-related outcomes is key to evaluating clinical progress
- High-quality documentation provides a record of medication response over consumers' lifetime
- Consumers and prescribers share in the decision-making process

Informed Medication Decisions

Mental health systems and agencies develop a systematic plan to ensure that decisions integrate the latest scientific evidence, consumer experience, and clinical expertise.

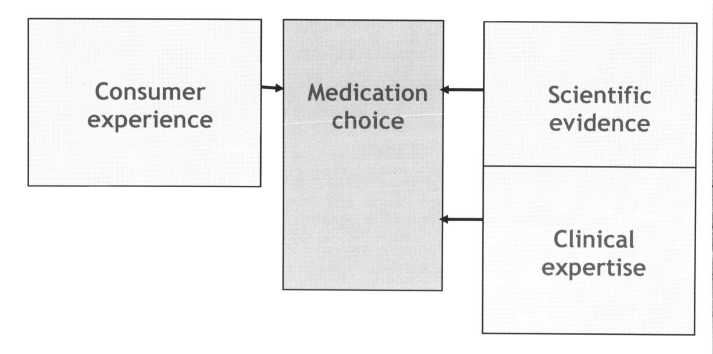

Team Approach
Consumers and prescribers work together with a team of practitioners to systematically gather the information needed for effective medication management.

Medication-Related Outcomes
The routine use of medication-related outcome measures helps prescribers and consumers evaluate whether medications have the desired effect.

High-Quality Documentation
Mental health systems and agencies evaluate current paperwork requirements and streamline documentation to ensure that the team has access to all information needed to make effective medication decisions.

Developing a systematic plan for high-quality documentation includes improving transferring information after visits to:
- Hospitals
- Emergency rooms
- General medical practitioners
- Other mental health providers

Shared Decision Making
Consumers are given information about their medications, share in the decision-making process, and are involved in evaluating their progress.

Systematic Plan for Medication Management

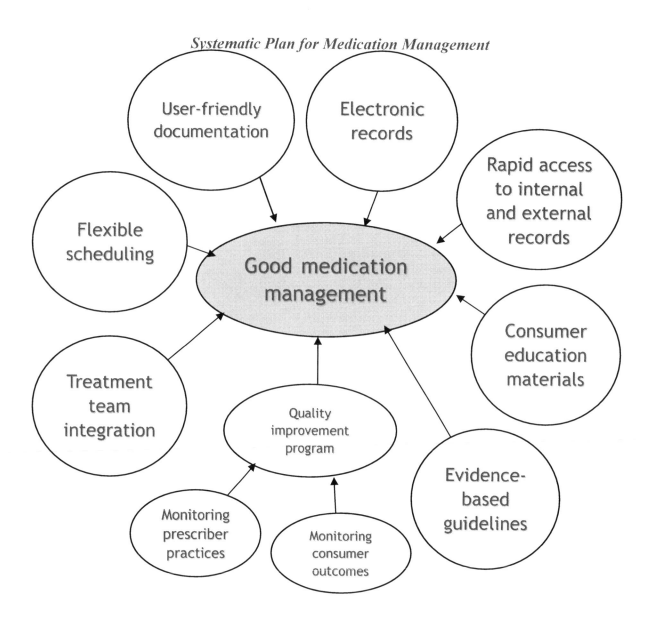

Module 9

LIVE YOUR LIFE NOT YOUR STORY

Excerpt from "Living Your Life, Not Your Story: A Guide for Helping the Helpers", 2nd Edition
– Richard D. Dávila and William B. Secor
Available for purchase on Amazon.com

There are many macro and micro organizations, both large and small, which provide services and helpers to their employees who are having problems. All of us, the ordinary citizen and those of us in the helping role, professionals and non-professionals, are often confronted with past events from our own lives. Helpers and students are often influenced or even devastated by events from their past: a death, PTSD, neglect, physical, emotional and sexual abuse, an accident, or a disability. It is true that past events can and do influence our lives. However, those past events cannot be changed, and therefore, it is the task of us and those helpers to live in the present, the now, and not allow themselves to become prisoners of their own personal past and past events.

Past events can be put in perspective, resolved in the present, so that the individual no longer is dominated by them, but can fully live his or her life in the present. This holds true for just everyday persons going through life. An incident or interaction creates a memory from the past and we find ourselves reacting to it as if that experience is in the present, when of course it is not. If we are not training ourselves to be in the present, we will continue to act and live our lives as if we are in the past, i.e., we will be an effect of our history, our story and not our present authentic life.

The Story – The Past
"Don't let yesterday use up too much of today." – Cherokee Proverb:

"With the past I have nothing to do; and with the future I live now" – Ralph Waldo Emerson

The past might be a nice place to visit occasionally, but one would not want to live there. There is a problem with the past and its memories – the story. It is not always remembered accurately.

What is the story? The story, for our purposes here, it is a narrative, based on assumed remembered past personal experiences, composed of recalled events which might or might not be accurate. Those recalled events can influence one's life positively or negatively. Obviously, past experiences can influence one's life, beliefs, emotions and actions. However, while they can influence, they should not dominate one's life. Life moves on and the individual must live in the now and must work to "be present."

Living in the past can have a corrosive effect for living in the present - a past could dominate the present and those who lived it. This is found and illustrated in many novels, poems, and films. Quite often, it is the creative artist who has considerably more understanding of the human condition than does the professional helper or care-giver.

Holistic
"Holistic refers to a Whole-Person Approach, addressing the body, mind, and spirit of individuals in the context of their lives." – *Healing Centers United (HCU), a Clearinghouse of Information about Holistic Healing Centers. (healingcenters.org)*

Triune Synergistic Model

New and Creative Way of Being	Present and Now	Past History: The Story
Vision ↻ New ↻ Creative	Here ↻ Now ↻ Present	Old ↻ Past ↻ History
• A different creative way • A change • A different and new vision • Creative to the present in the now • A consciousness into the present	• Our life is present and now • And now, and *now*, and *now* • One day at a time • In the moment • We need to be present **Bring consciousness into the moment**	• Stuck in our history/past • An effect of our history/past • The story lives, and *lives*, and *lives*!

The Synergy That Is Life

Consciousness means awareness of what is happening now. Consciousness gives you the ability to make new choices and start creating a new history right now. Your "now and present" is what's happening in and around you now. Your story is the past and your selective memory of the past.

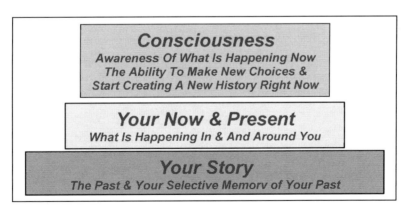

"You can clutch the past so tightly to your chest that is leaves your arms too full to embrace the present." *Jan Glidewell*

CONSCIENTIZATION
(Managing the Self)

- Even though history can carry wounds and is/was real at the time, we can choose to make a new history for tomorrow by living in the NOW.

- Taking responsibility for our current actions not being at effect of our past.

- Recognizing and accepting of the reality NOW is the first step in moving forward in life instead of being stuck in reverse.

Quotes Reflecting Bringing Consciousness in the Moment

"I have memories, but only a fool stores his past in the future." David Gerrold

"People are always asking about the good old days. I say, why don't you say the good now days?" Robert M. Young

"One problem with gazing too frequently into the past is that we may turn around to find the future has run out on us."
Michael Cibenko

"We can easily manage if we will only take, each day, the burden appointed to it. But the load will be too heavy for us if we carry yesterday's burden over again today, and then add the burden of the morrow before we are required to bear it."
John Newton

These quotes illustrate the importance of being in the present, the now. One of the ways this can happen is to bring consciousness to the present/the now. It is easy to be unconscious and just act off of whatever comes up for you. However, when that happens we end up spurting out things from the past and never get to the things of the now.

Practice being in the now, look at your shoes, look at what is before your eyes, and identify your current thoughts. Say, yesterday is a cancelled check, tomorrow is a promissory note, and TODAY is cash in hand. (Unknown author). Another important thing to keep in mind is to work at being an authentic person. Working at this helps us to stay present.

SELF-CARE

It is often said that one of the occupational hazards of being in the position of caring for others is neglecting care of ourselves. Yet, the old adage applies – we cannot give away something we don't have.

Wellness Self-Assessment

Using the self-assessment tool that looks at seven dimensions of wellness, simply rate yourself on the scale on the right side of the page. Please rate using the following scale

Always (5), Very Frequently (4), Frequently (3), Occasionally (2,), Almost Never (1), Never (0)

Physical Wellness Self-Assessment

1. I exercise for 30 minutes or more most days of the week. — 5 4 3 2 1 0
2. My exercise program includes activities that build my heart, muscles and flexibility. — 5 4 3 2 1 0
3. I select lean cuts of meat, poultry or fish — 5 4 3 2 1 0
4. I eat a variety of foods from all the food groups — 5 4 3 2 1 0
5. I eat breakfast — 5 4 3 2 1 0
6. I get an adequate amount of sleep (7 – 8 hours per night) — 5 4 3 2 1 0
7. I examine my breasts or testes once a month — 5 4 3 2 1 0
8. I participate in recommended periodic health screenings (blood pressure, etc.) — 5 4 3 2 1 0
9. I seek medical advice when needed — 5 4 3 2 1 0
10. I drink less than 5 alcoholic drinks at a sitting — 5 4 3 2 1 0
11. I avoid driving while under the influence of alcohol or drugs — 5 4 3 2 1 0
12. I avoid using tobacco products — 5 4 3 2 1 0

Emotional/Psychological Wellness Self-Assessment

1. I am able to sleep soundly throughout the night and wake feeling refreshed — 5 4 3 2 1 0
2. I am able to make decisions with a minimum of stress and worry.. — 5 4 3 2 1 0
3. I am able to set priorities — 5 4 3 2 1 0
4. I maintain a balance between school/work and personal life — 5 4 3 2 1 0

Spiritual Wellness Self-Assessment

1. I make time for relaxation in my day — 5 4 3 2 1 0
2. I make time in my day for prayer, meditation or personal time .. — 5 4 3 2 1 0
3. My values guide my actions and decisions — 5 4 3 2 1 0
4. I am accepting of the views of others — 5 4 3 2 1 0

Please rate using the following scale

Always (5), Very Frequently (4), Frequently (3), Occasionally (2,), Almost Never (1), Never (0)

Intellectual Wellness Self- Assessment

1. It is easy for me to apply knowledge from one situation to another — 5 4 3 2 1 0
2. I enjoy the amount and variety I read. — 5 4 3 2 1 0
3. I find life intellectually challenging and stimulating — 5 4 3 2 1 0
4. I obtain health information from reputable sources — 5 4 3 2 1 0
5. I spend money commensurate with my income, values and goals — 5 4 3 2 1 0
6. I pay bills in full each month (including my credit card) — 5 4 3 2 1 0

Occupational Wellness Self- Assessment

1. I am able to plan a manageable workload — 5 4 3 2 1 0
2. My career is consistent with my values and goals — 5 4 3 2 1 0
3. I earn enough money to meet my needs to provide stability for me and/or my family. — 5 4 3 2 1 0
4. My work benefits individuals and/or society — 5 4 3 2 1 0

Social Wellness Self- Assessment

1. I plan time to be with my family and friends — 5 4 3 2 1 0
2. I enjoy my time with others — 5 4 3 2 1 0
3. I am satisfied with the groups/organizations that I am a part of — 5 4 3 2 1 0
4. My relationships with others are positive and rewarding — 5 4 3 2 1 0
5. I explore diversity by interacting with people of other cultures, background and beliefs — 5 4 3 2 1 0

Environmental Wellness Self- Assessment

1. I minimize my exposure to second hand tobacco smoke — 5 4 3 2 1 0
2. I keep my vehicle maintained to ensure safety. — 5 4 3 2 1 0
3. When I see a safety hazard, I take steps to correct the problem — 5 4 3 2 1 0
4. I choose an environment that is free of excessive noise whenever possible — 5 4 3 2 1 0
5. I make efforts to reuse and recycle — 5 4 3 2 1 0
6. I try to create an environment that minimizes my stress — 5 4 3 2 1 0

SAMHSA – PERSONAL AND FAMILY WELLNESS

SAMHSA (Substance Abuse Mental Health Services Administration) states:
"We envision a future in which people with mental health and substance use disorders pursue optimal health, happiness, recovery and a full and satisfying life in the community via access to a range of effective services, support and resources"

Exercise – What is Wellness?

Describe what you consider to be a definition of wellness

Definition of Wellness

Wellness is not the absence of disease, illness or stress. It is much more than merely physical health, exercise or nutrition. It is the full integration of states of physical, mental, and spiritual well-being.

Wellness is:
- The presence of purpose in our lives.
- It is active involvement ins satisfying work and play.
- Wellness is joyful relationships,
- A healthy body and living environment.
- *Wellness is happiness.*

Aspects of Wellness

Aspects of wellness are overall well-being. Wellness incorporates these areas/aspects of a person's life: Physical, Environmental. Spiritual, Emotional/Psychological, Intellectual. Occupational, and Social.

Each facet can affect the overall quality of life. So, it is important to consider all these facets of your health.

8 Dimensions of SAMSHA's Wellness Initiative

1. Emotional – coping effectively with life and creating satisfying relationships.
2. Environmental – Good healthy by occupying pleasant, stimulating environments that support well-being.
3. Financial – satisfaction with current and future financial situations.
4. Intellectual – recognizing creative abilities and finding ways to expand knowledge and skill.
5. Occupational – personal satisfaction and enrichment from one's work.
6. Physical – recognizing the need for physical activity, healthy foods and sleep.
7. Social – developing a sense of connection, belonging and a well-developed support system.
8. Spiritual – expanding our sense of purpose and meaning in life.

Why Wellness Matters

People with mental health and substance use disorders die decades earlier than the general population, mostly due to preventable medical conditions:
- Diabetes
- Cardiovascular disease
- Respiratory disease
- Infectious diseases, including HIV

Risk factors for people with mental health and substance use disorders include:
- Trauma
- Social isolation

Other risk factors are:
- Tobacco
- Obesity
- Medication side effects

PERSONAL WELLNESS

- The "***Treater Should Be Treated***', i.e. to be effective as Coaches, Mentors, Peer Support Specialists, we need to maintain our wellness by working on and maintaining a self-care wellness plan of our own
- Only "a healthy mind can help another toward a healthy mind"
- You must choose what works for you
- Remember, intellectual stimulation is as important as the emotional, physical and spiritual aspects for your personal growth and wellness

THE RECOVERY WELLNESS PLAN

To support the recoveree in his or her recovery, it is a good idea for the recoveree to have a Recovery Wellness Plan. The plan addresses the following areas within a recoveree's life:
- Connectedness to the Recovery Community
- Physical Health
- Emotional Health
- Spiritual Health
- Living Accommodations
- School/Job/Education
- Personal Daily Living Management
- Any Other Area Identified by the Recoveree

One the next few pages, is the Recovery Wellness Plan, with some information about goal setting, that would be given to the recoveree.

However, as a Recovery Family Mentor, keep in mind the following:
- the plan is the recoveree's plan, not the Mentor's plan
- the recoveree writes, maintains and keeps the plan
- the recoveree and the Recovery Mentor may find it helpful for the recoveree to bring his/her plan with her/him to meetings with the Recovery Mentor.

RECOVERY WELLNESS PLAN (*For the Recoveree*)

This plan is written, maintained and kept by you, the recoveree. This is your plan.
It will be used in the conversations between you and your recovery coach/mentor. Bring it to meetings with your recovery coach/mentor.

Headings of the Recovery Wellness Plan include:
- Connectedness to the Recovery Community
- Physical Health
- Emotional Health
- Spiritual Health
- Living Accommodations
- School/Job/Education
- Personal Daily Living Management
- Any other areas you may want to include

Writing Smart Goals

When writing your goals, it is important to make sure that the goals that can be obtainable. Using this technique for writing goals can be very helpful when creating goals with the Recovery Wellness Plan.

Specific	Define Expectations. Avoid generalities and use verbs to start the sentence
Measurable	Establish concrete criteria for measuring progress toward the attainment of each goal you set. Quality, Quantity, timeliness.
Achievable	Challenging goals within reason. Do not assign too many goals though each one is within reason
Realistic	A goal must represent an objective toward which you are both willing and able to work. A goal can be both high and realistic.
Time-bound	Date or elapsed time to complete the goal

WHAT IS MY OVERALL RECOVERY WELLNESS GOAL?

It is often helpful to break down recovery wellness into smaller parts; these will be listed on the following pages below. Under each heading, you will find some questions to get you thinking? Some will strike you as more important than others. Pay attention to these. There is an opportunity to make a goal under each heading, yet you do not need to have a goal under each heading. Oftentimes, it gets confusing to have more than a couple of goals at a time.

1. Connection to the Recovery Community

- Do I have contact on a regular basis with people in recovery?
- Am I or do I want to be involved in a recovery support group?
- If involved in a support group, am I active in it and taking suggestions?
- Am I or do I want to be involved with a faith community?
- If involved in a faith community, am I active in that community?
- Do I spend social time with others in recovery?
- Other questions I should be asking myself?

Recovery Goal

Steps I need to take to reach my goal

Who else might be involved?

When do I want to have this goal accomplished?

2. Physical Health

- Do I eat a balanced diet?
- Do I exercise regularly?
- Do I get enough sleep?
- Do I need to see a doctor or a dentist?
- Do my health care providers know that I am in recovery?
- If I have been prescribed medication for my physical health, am I taking it as

Recovery Goal

Steps I need to take to reach my goal

Who else might be involved?

When do I want to have this goal accomplished?

3. Emotional Health

- Do I work at being in healthy relationships?
- Am I seeing a therapist/counselor or need to be seeing one?
- Do my health care providers know that I am in recovery?
- If I have been prescribed medication for my physical health, am I taking it as prescribed?
- Other questions I should be asking myself?

Recovery Goal

Steps I need to take to reach my goal

Who else might be involved?

When do I want to have this goal accomplished?

4. Spiritual Health

- Am I comfortable with my spirituality?
- Do I need to develop a spiritual sense and spiritual practices?
- Am I disciplined about my spiritual practices?
- Do I take time each day for prayer, meditation and/or personal reflection?
- Any other questions I should be asking myself?

Recovery Goal

Steps I need to take to reach my goal

Who else might be involved?

When do I want to have this goal accomplished?

5. Living Accommodations

- Does where I live support my recovery?
- Does whom I live with support my recovery?
- Do I need to make any changes in my living situation?
- Any other questions I should be asking myself?

Recovery Goal

Steps I need to take to reach my goal

Who else might be involved?

When do I want to have this goal accomplished?

6. Job/Education

- Do I have or need a job?
- Does my job support my recovery goals?
- Am I satisfied with my education status?
- Do I need to return to some form of education?
- Do I need training on any area?
- Any other questions I should be asking myself?

Recovery Goal

Steps I need to take to reach my goal

Who else might be involved?

When do I want to have this goal accomplished?

7. Personal Daily Living Management

- Do I have a way to manage my money? Checking account?
- Do I know how to use and balance a checkbook?
- If I have credit, do I manage it appropriately?
- Do I pay all my bills on time?
- Do I save any money?
- Any other questions I should be asking myself?

Recovery Goal

Steps I need to take to reach my goal

Who else might be involved?

When do I want to have this goal accomplished?

8. Other

- Are there any other areas I wish to explore?

Recovery Goal

Steps I need to take to reach my goal

Who else might be involved?

When do I want to have this goal accomplished?

SECTION THREE SLIDES

Behavioral Health Mentor Training

Day 3

Trainers: Richard D Dávila, Ph.D.
Jackie Sue Griffin, MBA, MS

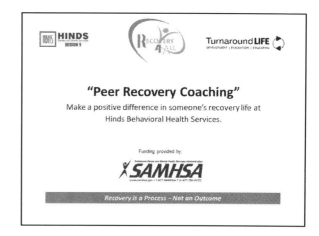

"Peer Recovery Coaching"

Make a positive difference in someone's recovery life at Hinds Behavioral Health Services.

Funding provided by:

SAMHSA

Recovery is a Process — Not an Outcome

Behavioral Health is Essential To Health

Prevention Works

Treatment is Effective

People Recover

Today's Agenda

- Welcome, Agenda and Reconnection
- Ethics
- Fragility
- Defining Culture and Cultural Competency
- Power Shuffle
- Medication Management
- Live Your Life Not Your Story
- Recovery Wellness Plan
- **All Recovery Meeting**

Ethics

Please take a few moments to write your personal definition of Ethics

Now let's come up with a group definition.

Ethics

According to Merriam Webster ...

Ethics are rules of behavior based on ideas about what is morally good and bad.

For RC and CPSS, ethics are:

- A set of developed and accepted standards or principles of behaviors and actions for both individuals and organizations within a profession.
- A standard code of behavior that is created to enhance service provision and create a climate of dignity and respect
- An agreed upon set of morals, values and conduct standards accepted by the group

Common Definitions

Let's write a simple definition for each of these terms:

- Principle
- Morals
- Values

Common Definitions

- Principles – Fundamental truths, laws, doctrine, or motivating forces upon which others are based; a rule of conduct. e.g. Above all, do no harm.
- Morals – Principles with respect to right or wrong in conduct.
- Values – Social principles, goals, or standards held by an individual, group or society.

Common Definitions

Fiduciary – is a term describing relationships in which one person has assumed a special duty and obligation for the care of another.

- The relationship of coach/mentor to recoveree is not one of equal power
- It is a relationship where one party has a higher degree of vulnerability
- Therefore, there is a higher level of obligation than in fully reciprocal relationships

Common Definitions

Boundary Management – encompasses the decisions that increase or decrease intimacy within a relationship.

- In more professional relationships, the hierarchical boundaries are more pronounced and are governed by maintaining detachment and distance
- Peer-based recovery support services rely on reciprocity and minimizing social distance
- While both services affirm boundaries of inappropriateness, these boundaries may differ

Common Definitions

Multi Party Vulnerability – is a phrase that conveys how multiple parties can be injured by what a RC/CPSS does or fails to do.

- This may include the recoveree, family members, organizations, the larger community of support services, the recovery community and the community at large.

Ethics in Recovery Coaching and Peer Support Specialist Mentoring

A Recovery Coach/Peer Support Specialist is anyone interested in promoting recovery by removing barriers and obstacles to recovery by serving as a personal guide and mentor for people seeking or in recovery.

- Motivator and Cheerleader
- Ally and Confidant
- Truth Teller
- Role Model and Mentor
- Problem Solver
- Resource Broker
- Advocate
- Community Organizer
- Friend and Companion
- Lifestyle Consultant

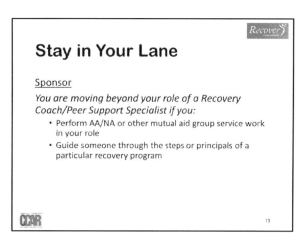
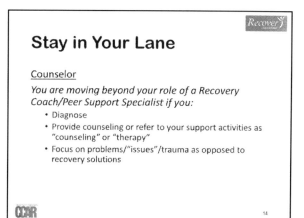
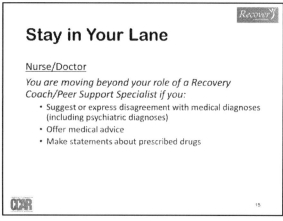
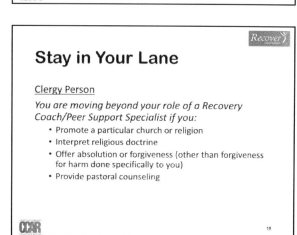
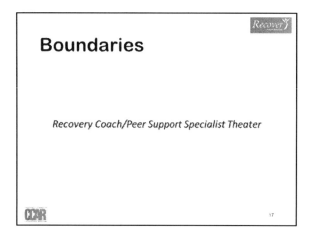
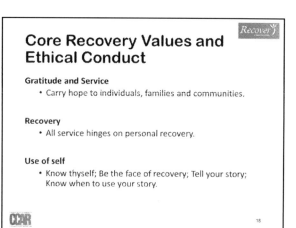

Core Recovery Values and Ethical Conduct

Capability
- Improve yourself; give your best.

Honesty
- Tell the truth; Separate fact from opinion; When wrong, admit it.

Authenticity of Voice
- Accurately represent your recovery experience and the role from which you are speaking

Core Recovery Values and Ethical Conduct

Credibility
- Walk what you talk.

Fidelity
- Keep your promises.

Humility
- Work within the limitations of your experience and role.

Core Recovery Values and Ethical Conduct

Loyalty
- Don't give up; offer multiple chances.

Hope
- Offer self and others as living proof; Focus on the positive – strengths, assets, and possibilities rather than problems and pathology.

Dignity and Respect
- Express compassion; Accept imperfection; Honor each other's potential.

Core Recovery Values and Ethical Conduct

Acceptance
- "The roads to recovery are many" (Wilson, 1944); Learn about diverse pathways and styles of recovery.

Autonomy and Choice
- Recovery is voluntary; It must be chosen; Enhance choices and choice making.

Discretion
- Respect privacy; Don't gossip.

Core Recovery Values and Ethical Conduct

Protection
- Do no harm; Do not exploit; Protect others; Avoid conflicts of interest.

Advocacy
- Challenge injustice; Be a voice for the voiceless; Empower others to speak.

Stewardship
- Use resources wisely.

Ethics

REMEMBER

- To Always Stay in Your Lane

- Always, when in Doubt, Check with your Supervisor

Recovery Management and
Recovery-Oriented Systems of Care:
Scientific Rationale and Promising Practices
William L. White, MA
Senior Research Consultant
Chestnut Health Systems
2008

Fragility of Post-treatment Recovery

Individuals leaving addiction treatment are fragilely balanced between recovery and re-addiction in the hours, days, weeks, months, and years following discharge.

Fragility of Post-treatment Recovery

- These individuals are making recovery and re-addiction decisions during a time in which treatment specialists have disengaged from their lives, but many sources of recovery sabotage are present.
- To state that early post-treatment recovery is fragile is not to say that long-term recovery is not possible.

Fragility of Post-treatment Recovery

The recovery prevalence rate for persons meeting lifetime criteria for substance use disorders ranges between 50-60%.

Fifty percent of AA members surveyed report six or more years of recovery, and

51% of people self-identified as "in recovery" in the larger community also report recovery duration of six or more years.

Fragility of Post-treatment Recovery

Factors related to post-treatment relapse of adults and adolescents include craving, interpersonal conflict, emotional distress, social pressure to use from peers, exposure to alcohol/drug-using environments, initial use of a drug other than drug of choice, and a lessening in vigilance and recovery maintenance activities.

Fragility of Post-treatment Recovery

Relapse is often embedded in the social interactions that occur after treatment support is withdrawn.

There are two dimensions to such interactions:
- contact and communication with active users
  and
- contact and communication with non-addicts.

The risk of relapse is high when:
- the former offers a siren call to return to a world where so many of the addict's prior needs were met,
  and
- the latter includes expressions of hostility, skepticism, and distrust.

Fragility of Post-treatment Recovery

A meta-analysis of opiate treatment outcome research found post-treatment relapse associated:
- with high levels of pre-treatment drug use
- prior treatment,
- the lack of a prior period of abstinence,
- abstinence from alcohol,
- depression,
- high levels of stress,
- unemployment,
- association with drug using peers,
- shorter length of treatment, and leaving treatment prior to completion.

Alcohol often plays a role in post-treatment relapse, regardless of drug of choice prior to treatment entry.

Defining Culture and Cultural Competence

Exercise: Culture & Cultural Competence Definitions

In your small groups come up with definitions for both Culture and Cultural Competence.

<u>Challenge yourself to do so with a complete sentence and without the use of bullets.</u>

Definition of Culture

- Culture generally refers to "shared values, norms, traditions, customs, art, history, folklore and institutions of a group of people." (Orlandi, Weston, & Epstein, 1992)

Definition of Cultural Competence

- A set of behaviors, attitudes and policies
- that come together in a system, agency, or
- program or among individuals, enabling
- them to function effectively in diverse
- cultural interactions and similarities within,
- among, and between groups."
- *U.S. Department of Health and Human Services*

Definition of Cultural Competence

- Cultural Competence is a point on a continuum that represents the *POLICIES and PRACTICES of an organization,* or the VALUES and
- BEHAVIOR of an individual which enable that organization or person to interact effectively in a culturally diverse environment.

Medication, Treatment, Evaluation, and Management
MedTEAM
An Evidence-Based Practice

What Are Evidence-Based Practices?

Services that have consistently demonstrated their *effectiveness* in helping people with mental illness achieve their desired goals

Effectiveness was established by different people who conducted rigorous studies and obtained similar outcomes

Examples of Evidence-Based Practices

- Peer Support
- Assisted Outpatient Treatment (AOT)
- Medication, Treatment, Evaluation, and Management (MedTEAM)
- Assertive Community Treatment
- Family Psychoeducation
- Illness Management and Recovery
- Integrated Treatment for Co-Occurring Disorders
- Supported Employment

Why Implement Evidence-Based Practices?

According to the New Freedom Commission on Mental Health:

State-of-the-art treatments, based on decades of research, are not being transferred from research to community settings

Why Implement Evidence-Based Practices?
(continued)

According to the New Freedom Commission on Mental Health:

If effective treatments were more efficiently delivered through our mental health services system ... millions of Americans would be more successful in school, at work, and in their communities

What Is MedTEAM?

MedTEAM is a systematic, evidence-based approach for offering medication management to people with mental illnesses

It helps those who prescribe medications to integrate the best current research evidence, clinical expertise, and consumer experience

Practice Principles of MedTEAM

- The latest scientific evidence guides medication decisions
- Medication management requires a team approach
- Systematically assessing medication-related outcomes is key to evaluating clinical progress
- High-quality documentation provides a record of medication response over consumers' lifetime
- Consumers and prescribers share in the decisionmaking process

Informed Medication Decisions

Mental health systems and agencies develop a systematic plan to ensure that decisions integrate the latest scientific evidence, consumer experience, and clinical expertise

Informed Medication Decisions

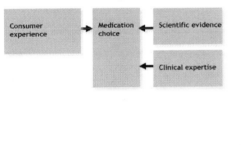

Team Approach

Consumers and prescribers work together with a team of practitioners to systematically gather the information needed for effective medication management

Medication-related Outcomes

The routine use of medication-related outcome measures helps prescribers and consumers evaluate whether medications have the desired effect

High-Quality Documentation

Mental health systems and agencies evaluate current paperwork requirements and streamline documentation to ensure that the team has access to all information needed to make effective medication decisions

High-Quality Documentation

Developing a systematic plan for high-quality documentation includes improving transferring information after visits to:

- Hospitals
- Emergency rooms
- General medical practitioners
- Other mental health providers

Shared Decision Making

Consumers are given information about their medications, share in the decision making process, and are involved in evaluating their progress

Systematic Plan for Medication Management

Summary

Effective medication management requires integrating the best current research evidence, clinical expertise, and consumer experience into the decision making process

MedTEAM offers an evidence-based approach to help mental health systems and agencies develop systematic plans to guide medication management

Additional Resources

For more information about MedTEAM and other evidence-based practices, visit:

Live YOUR Life
Not YOUR Story

Developed & Copyright by,
Richard D. Davila, Ph.D., 2006
Distinguished Professor of Humanics, Springfield College

HOLISTIC

"Holistic refers to a "Whole" Person Approach Addressing the Body – Mind – Spirit of Individuals in the Context of Their Lives"

Healing Centers United (HCU), a Clearinghouse of Information about Holistic Healing Centers.
(healingcenters.org)

Triune Synergistic Model

New Creative   Present Now   Past History

Past History *(The Story)*

- Stuck in Our History/Past
- At Effect of Our History/Past
- The Story **Lives** & **Lives** & **Lives**

Past History *(The Story)*

Old → Past → History (cycle)

Present & Now

Our Life is Present & Now

And **Now** And **Now** And **Now**

One Day at a Time

In the Moment

Need to be Present

Bring Consciousness into the Moment

Present & Now

Here → Now → Present (cycle)

The Old Story Invades

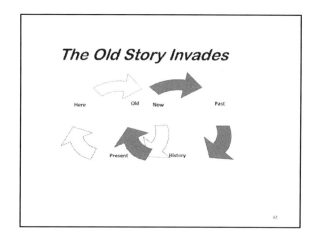

New & Creative Way of Being

- A Different Creative Way
- A Change
- A Different & New Vision
- Creative to the Present in the Now
- A Consciousness into the Present

Bring Consciousness into the Moment

The New & Creative

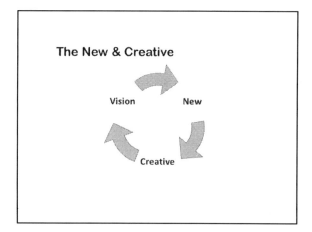

The Synergy

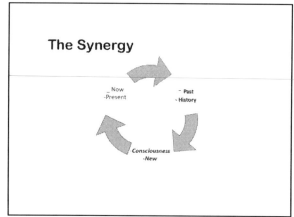

The Synergy That Is Life

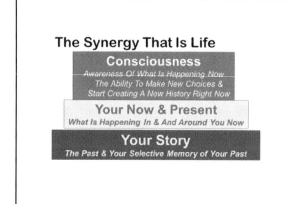

QUOTE

- With the past, I have nothing to do; nor with the future. I live now.

- Ralph Waldo Emerson

QUOTE

- You can clutch the past so tightly to your chest that it leaves your arms too full to embrace the present.

  - Jan Glidewell

QUOTE

- I have memories – but only a fool store his past in the future.

  - David Gerrold

QUOTE

- Don't let yesterday use up too much of today.

  - Cherokee Indian Proberb

QUOTE

- People are always asking about the good old days. I say, why don't you say the good now days?

  - Robert M. Young

New & Creative Way of Being

- A Different Creative Way
- A Change
- A Different & New Vision
- Creative to the Present in the Now
- A Consciousness into the Present

Bring *Consciousness* into the Moment

Our Story
Teaches Us How To Act

- "Mental models" are deeply ingrained assumptions, generalizations, or even pictures or images that influence how we understand the world and how we take action."

Being Conscious Of Our Story
In The Now

Working With Mental Models Involves Learning To ...
- *Turn The Mirror Inward*
- *Unearth Our Internal Pictures Of The World*
- *Bring Them To The Surface*
- *Hold Them Rigorously To Scrutiny."*

Being Conscious Of Our Story
In The Now

It also includes the ability to carry on "learningful" conversations that
- *balance inquiry and advocacy, where people expose their own thinking effectively and make that thinking open to the influence of others.*

QUOTE

- **One problem with gazing too frequently into the past is that we may turn around to find the future has run out on us.**

- Michael Cibenko

QUOTE

- **Living in the past is dull and lonely business; looking back stains the neck muscles, causing you to bump into people not going your way.**

- Edna Ferber

Being Conscious Of Our Story
In The Now

RamDass (Richard Alpert) author of, "Be Here Now" Below is a small excerpt out of his latest book, "Still Here";

- "It is widely believed that the state of consciousness at the moment of death affects the trajectory of our reincarnation."
- "if we do not reincarnate we will at least have lived and died in a worthy manner".

Conscientization
(Managing The Self)

- Even though history can carry wounds and is/*was* real at the time, we can choose to make a new history for tomorrow by living in the NOW.
- Taking responsibility for our *current* actions not being at effect of our past.
- Recognizing and accepting of the reality NOW is the first step in moving forward in life instead of being stuck in reverse.

QUOTE

- The Past is the textbook of tyrants the Future the Bible of the Free. Those who are solely governed by the Past stand like Lot's wife, crystallized in the act of looking backward, and forever incapable of looking before.

- Herman Melville, *White Jacket*

QUOTE

- We can easily manage if we will only take, each day, the burden appointed to it. But the load will be too heavy for us if we carry yesterday's burden over again today, and then add the burden of the morrow before we are required to bear it.

- John Newton

Personal Reflection
"What The Hell, It Really Did Happen!"

In November, 2006 as I sit in a sweat lodge with a Medicine Man and my stepson on the grounds of the Navajo Nation in New Mexico, I hear the words of the Medicine Man come forth, he states:

Personal Reflection
"What The Hell, It Really Did Happen!"

- "being here and present is an opportunity to get rid of our stressors and history that continues to keep us stressed"

- He then states, the effect of getting rid of these stressors will or can be felt within hours, days, weeks.

Personal Reflection
"What The Hell, It Really Did Happen!"

- What the previous slide suggests to me is that living in the moment allows for the release of the *"at effect history"* in our lives. These are the things in our past that we act on in our *"now space"*.

- We do not need to be in a sweat lodge for this release process to occur in our lives.

QUOTE

- The ability to be in the present moment is a major component of mental wellness.

- Abraham Maslow

Self-Care

Treater Should Be Treated

WELLNESS SELF-ASSESSMENT

It is often said that one of the occupational hazards of being in the position of caring for others is neglecting care of ourselves. Yet, the old adage applies – we cannot give away something we don't have.

WELLNESS SELF-ASSESSMENT

Using the self-assessment tool that looks at seven dimensions of wellness, simply rate yourself on the scale on the right side of the page. Please rate using the following scale
- Always (5)
- Very Frequently (4)
- Frequently (3)
- Occasionally (2)
- Almost Never (1)
- Never (0)

PERSONAL WELLNESS

- The "*Treater Should Be Treated*", i.e. to be effective as Coaches, Mentors, Peer Support Specialists, we need to maintain our wellness by working on and maintaining a self-care wellness plan of our own
- Only "a healthy mind can help another toward a healthy mind"
- You must choose what works for you

Remember
Intellectual stimulation is as important as the emotional, physical and spiritual aspects for your personal growth and wellness

---

PERSONAL WELLNESS

Please refer to your manuals for additional material about the dimensions of wellness from SAMHSA and a study from University of California, Riverside.

You can use this information for ongoing self-care.

Recovery Wellness Plan

Recovery Wellness Plan

To support the recoveree in his or her recovery, it is a good idea for the recoveree to have a Recovery Wellness Plan. The plan addresses the following areas within a recoveree's life:
- Connectedness to the Recovery Community
- Physical Health
- Emotional Health
- Spiritual Health
- Living Accommodations
- School/Job/Education
- Personal Daily Living Management
- Any Other Area Identified by the Recoveree

Recovery Wellness Plan

- However, as a Certified Peer Support Specialist (CPSS), keep in mind the following:

  - the plan is the recoveree's plan, not the CPSS's plan
  - the recoveree writes, maintains and keeps the plan
  - the recoveree and the CPSS may find it helpful for the recoveree to bring his/her plan to sessions with the CPSS

All Recovery Meeting

End Module Three Slides

This page left intentionally blank

APPENDIX

Journal Pages

JOURNAL

JOURNAL

JOURNAL

JOURNAL

ALL RECOVERY MEETING

Opening

Hello everyone. Welcome to this All-Recovery meeting. My name is _____. An All-Recovery meeting welcomes all who struggle with addiction, are affected by addiction and/or support the recovery lifestyle. An All-Recovery meeting is "non-denominational", meaning all pathways of recovery are embraced here. Today, I will choose a universal recovery topic and then we will discuss it. Specifically, an All-Recovery meeting is not affiliated with any "Anonymous" program although we are likely to hear comments associated with 12-Step fellowships. Coming from a place of mutual respect and understanding, let's observe some basic meeting agreements.

1. Please respect the opinions and remarks of others.
2. Please no cross talking; only one person speaks at a time.
3. Please turn your cell phones off or place them on vibrate.
4. Please refrain from the overuse of profanity in order not to offend others.

Are there any announcements?

Let's begin by introducing ourselves to one another, how you introduce yourself is completely up to you. Again, my name is _____ and I am _____.
{You might consider saying, "I am a person in long-term recovery and for me that means...}

This is a topic discussion meeting and the topic I have chosen is _____. You may share on this topic (or not) or on something else that relates to recovery. Please be mindful of the amount of people in the room and our time frame when sharing.
{Start the sharing with some thoughts on the meeting topic. When finished say something like, "That's it for me, who'd like to share?" As best you can, refrain from commenting on other people's sharing, the less you say as facilitator, the better.}

Closing

In closing, I would like to thank you all for coming today. We close an All-Recovery meeting with a positive affirmation about ourselves followed by a moment of silence to remember why we are here.
{Start this by giving a positive affirmation like "I'm proud of my recovery today", "Life is good today". After everyone has shared, offer a moment of silence then, close by saying "Thank you".}

All-Recovery Meeting Format©
Updated March 2016

Biographies

RICHARD D. DÁVILA, ACSW, Ph. D

Dr. Dávila is a Recovery Life Coach Professional who helps individuals seeking regular ongoing coaching and/or recovery support as people in recovery build a solid foundation. He is the President of Recovery All, Inc. a company that focuses on Recovery Support Services for all pathways to recovery.

Dr. Dávila has been International/National Certified Gambling Counselor, Licensed Clinical Social Worker and a Certified Alcohol and Drug Abuse Counselor. Currently he is a Recovery Coach Professional, Trainer and Trainer of Trainers (TOT) for the CCAR Recovery Coach Academy. He is renowned international lecturer in adult education, alcohol & drugs, and diversity.

Dr. Dávila received his Master's (MSW) and Ph.D. from the University of Connecticut. With more than thirty-five years of experience in education, addictions training, and community work, Dr. Dávila brings unparalleled experience and expertise in the Addiction and Recovery Studies field.

Dr. Dávila has held faculty and management positions in the fields of addiction studies and educational leadership. He has served on local, state, and national agency boards in the field of addictions, including Initial Review Groups (IRG) for the office of Substance Abuse and Mental Health Services Administration (SAMHSA).

He is the co-author of three books: "Living Your Life Not Your Story, (2nd edition) "A Holistic Look at Substance Use Recovery; a book to encourage the recovery wellness model", and "Recovery Family Mentor Workbook". All can be ordered through www.Amazon.com. He has also written numerous articles for respected academic addiction journals. Further, Dr. Dávila has presented at several national addiction conferences.

Dr. Dávila served as the Associate Dean for the School of Human Services for Springfield College. And, for the 2006-2007 academic year, was appointed Distinguished Professor of Humanics, the highest faculty distinction as a faculty person at Springfield College.

Recently, Dr. Dávila retired after 33.5 years of service from his position as Professor and Campus Director at Springfield College, serving as a full, tenured professor for the School of Professional and Continuing Studies, Tampa Bay Florida Campus. Springfield College, He is currently Professor Emeritus   He is also currently helping treatment programs implement enhanced "recovery support services". He is a sought-after *Recovery Life Coach* and a deliverer of quality training to persons wishing to become a Recovery Coach Professional (RCP) and a Certified Recovery Support Specialist (CRSS) as well as other addiction studies courses.

He is a person in long term recovery.

JACKIE SUE GRIFFIN, MBA, MS, BA

Ms. Griffin has an MBA with a concentration in nonprofit management and a Master of Science degree in Organizational Management and Leadership from Springfield College School of Professional and Continuing Studies. She holds 26 years of experience dealing with small businesses ownership, overseeing operations, grant management, grant development, fundraising and nonprofit management. Primary responsibilities include leading grant development and implementing high-level program design and systems change strategies and facilitating communication between key stakeholders. She is a Certified Recovery Coach and trainer and former journalist mastering all forms of written and oral communications. Specific expertise involves extensive experience dealing with small businesses ownership, overseeing operations, grant and contract management and procurement, grant and contract development and nonprofit management.

Over the past 14 years, Ms. Griffin has partnered with Turnaround Life and Turnaround Achievement Network securing more than $63 million in government grants and expanding systems of care and behavioral health treatment in Florida, Mississippi and New Orleans. Ms. Griffin's responsibilities include grant development and developing and implementing high-level program design and systems change strategies and serving as evaluation director. Responsibilities include developing and implementing high-level program design and systems change strategies and advising leadership teams. She is a Certified Recovery Coach and trainer and former journalist mastering all forms of written and oral communications.

Ms. Griffin has proven competencies in Strategic Prevention Framework, facilitating community assessment, planning, implementation and evaluation, strategic planning, advocacy, policy analysis, grant writing and grant management, systems transformation, and evaluation. Evidence-based program design expertise includes coalition development, substance abuse prevention, addictions and co-occurring disorders treatment, suicide prevention, adult and children's mental health systems of care and recovery-oriented systems of care. Ms. Griffin is the Executive Director and sole owner of Jackie Sue Griffin & Associates, LLC. She founded the company in 2013 to provide nonprofit organizations, government agencies and health and human services businesses expertise in fund development and philanthropy. Her expertise includes grant management and developments, training for health care clients and nonprofit organizations, advocacy, and policy development.

Ms. Griffin has taught undergraduate and graduate students at Springfield College School of Professional and Continuing Studies, Tampa Bay campus as an adjunct instructor for 15 years. She is the President of the Community Advisory Board for Springfield. Ms. Griffin earned her Bachelor of Arts degree in Writing and English from the University of Tampa. She received a four-year academic scholarship to pay for her undergraduate studies.

MARGUERITE (RITA) BALLARD, R.C., RFM, CRRA
Editor

Ms. Ballard is a trained Recovery Coach, Recovery Family Mentor, Certified Recovery Resident Administrator, and a trained Instructor for the CCAR, Recovery Family Mentor and Recovery Coaching Concepts curriculum. She has had a variety of experiences in developing training curriculum and delivering education and training seminars.

Her experience includes:
- Providing Recovery Coach and Recovery Family Mentor services to individuals seeking support and education in their recovery journey
- Assisting in the creation, editing and production of training materials in the field of Recovery,
- Creating technical training materials, exercises and job aids for classroom instruction
- Providing technical and educational support in various software solutions to user communities.
- Producing assessments for certification and course work completion

Ms. Ballard is a person in long-term recovery.

Acknowledgements

Dávila, Richard, D., MSW, Ph.D.
Galer, Michal Mendel, Ph.D.
Jackie Sue Griffin, MBA, MS, BA
Terry Gorski
Ballard, Marguerite "Rita", RC, RFM, CRRA
Wegscheider-Cruse, Sharon, MSW
National Association for Children Of Alcoholics (NACOA)
Connecticut Community for Addiction Recovery (CCAR)
Substance Abuse Mental Health Services Administration (SAMHSA)
National Council on Alcoholism and Drug Dependency (NCADD)
Ablett, Mitch, PhD
Gillette, Russel, LPC, LADC
Bowen, Murray, MD
Right Response - *http://rightresponse.org/my/*

Made in United States
Orlando, FL
13 December 2024